BIRDS

— OF —

SOUTH-EAST ASIA

A Photographic Guide to the Birds
of Thailand, Malaysia, Singapore,
the Philippines and Indonesia

MORTEN STRANGE

NH
NEW
HOLLAND

First published in 1998 by
New Holland (Publishers) Ltd
London • Cape Town • Sydney • Singapore

24 Nutford Place
London W1H 6DQ
United Kingdom

80 McKenzie Street
Cape Town 8001
South Africa

3/2 Aquatic Drive
Frenchs Forest, NSW 2086
Australia

ISBN 1 85368 879 7

Commissioning editor: Jo Hemmings

Edited, typeset and designed by D & N Publishing, Membury Business Park
Lambourn Woodlands, Hungerford, Berkshire

Reproduction by Pica Colour Separation Overseas (Pte) Ltd
Printed and bound in Singapore by Tien Wah Press (Pte) Ltd

Photographic acknowledgements:
All the photographs in this book were taken by Morten Strange, except for:
Ng Bee Choo 100c, Goran Ekstrom/Windrush Photos (101), Brenda Holcombe/Windrush Photos
(25tr), Frank Lambert (21tr, 21br, 58b), Pete Morris (32tr, 36tl, 57c, 58tl, 59r, 59bl, 80tr, 88t,
106, 107), Alan Ow Yong (24t, 56b, 59c, 86tr), Ong Kiem Sian (19b, 20b, 21tl, 22b, 23br,
53c, 82r), David Tipling/Windrush Photos (26tr), Uthai Treesucon (37, 42tl, 56tr, 59t, 59br,
87b, 100b), Anders Trevad (25b), Arnoud B. van den Berg/Windrush Photos (100t) and Adisak
Vidhidharm (50t).

Previous page: Green Bee-eater *(Merops orientalis)*.

Opposite: Yellow-vented Bulbul *(Pycnonotus goiavier)*.

CONTENTS

Olive-backed Sunbird (Nectarinia jugularis), male.

FOREWORD

From 1990 to 1992, I chaired the Preparatory Committee for the United Nations Conference on Environment and Development, often referred to as the Earth Summit. I also chaired the Main Committee at Rio de Janeiro. This meeting became a watershed in international politics because, for the first time, environmental protection was seen as an integral part of development by the whole international community.

In the natural environment, birds are a class of animals that are relatively easy to observe. We all enjoy watching the pretty and active creatures in our gardens and parks. More elusive species, however, can only live and be found in remote places like offshore islands and large expanses of primary rainforest.

Birds react quickly to changes in their surroundings and are therefore good indicators of the health of the environment. Surveys have shown that where you have a sound population of birds, other life-forms thrive as well.

This new guide for the first time provides a photographic introduction to all the most important bird families found in the South-east Asian region.

Nothing is more important on our planet than to protect the natural world because, as far as we know, ours is the only one in the Universe with life. This natural wonder must not be damaged. However, most people also strive for a better life, and rightly so. So to ensure continued economic development and progress and at the same time protect and conserve the earth's biological diversity will be our generation's biggest challenge. Take a look at the outstanding beauty and variety of the bird life of South-east Asia as presented in this book for inspiration.

PROFESSOR TOMMY KOH
Ambassador-at-Large
Ministry of Foreign Affairs, Singapore
Patron, The Nature Society (Singapore)

$\textbf{\textit{1}}$ NTRODUCTION

Moving into a new area and exploring how the bird life differs from what you are used to is one of the greater joys of birdwatching. If visiting South-east Asia for the first time, there will be hundreds of new birds for you to see, as there are simply so many birds here that do not occur anywhere else. Even if you are a resident in the region, it is easy to find new birds without travelling too far from your home.

Area Covered
This book can only be a short introduction to the rich and varied bird life of South-east Asia. For the purposes of the book, the area covered can be defined as the part of the Oriental region made up of Thailand, across Malaysia, Singapore, the Philippines and all of Indonesia apart from Irian Jaya. These were also the countries that founded the Association of South-east Asian Nations (ASEAN) in 1967, an organization that has since grown considerably in size and influence.

In zoogeographical terms, the Oriental region, since 1988 also known as the Indomalayan region, is an area that stretches from Pakistan in the west to Borneo in the east. Southern China and Taiwan constitute the northern limit. East of Borneo and between Bali and Lombok runs the imaginary Wallace's Line, east of which the animal and plant life changes significantly. However, since many bird families with Oriental affinities extend across this line, the Lydekker's Line further east near Irian Jaya is a more definitive demarcation; east of here a new region begins in earnest, the Australasian region. The area between the two lines is called the Wallacea subregion and holds many species of birds found nowhere else, so-called endemics. Many species are also endemic to the Sunda subregion, a cross-national section made up of southern Thailand, Peninsular Malaysia, Sumatra, Borneo and Java.

A Wealth of Birds
South-east Asia is one of the richest places in the world for birds. It is also one of the most enjoyable places to go travelling, with a friendly and gracious human population that makes visiting a pleasure. Nevertheless, the natural world here is still relatively poorly known. Most people in the area have been too busy pushing forward economically and socially to care about wild birds – and they have been pretty successful at that! This is about to change; there is a growing appreciation of nature in general and the wild bird population in particular amongst residents and visitors to South-east Asia, and it is hoped that this book will contribute to fuelling this interest.

Birdwatching can be enjoyed for many reasons and in many ways, but two factors are universal: all birdwatchers appreciate the beauty of birds and the freedom of movement they represent. The aesthetic aspects of this hobby-cum-science should not be neglected; for example, the thrill of suddenly seeing an attractive and elusive bird either feeding at close quarters or flying through its natural habitat. Therefore the pictures in this book have been selected deliberately to convey these feelings.

Another element to birdwatching is 'collecting'. Most birdwatchers start by watching birds near their home in a garden, park or perhaps on a local lake. As they become familiar with the common species they move further afield to find new birds. Some develop a seemingly compulsive urge, and before they know it they have become roaming 'twitchers', trying to add new species to their world list. As there are some 9,300 birds in the world, this is a never-ending task.

Climatic and Habitat Differences Across the Region

Bird life changes with different climates. If you want to find new species, the hot and humid equatorial rainforests of South-east Asia have the highest diversity of any habitat. Despite this abundance, the lowland rainforest is probably the most challenging habitat for birdwatchers, since viewing

Below: Primary rainforest and a resthouse on the beautiful island of Halmahera in eastern Indonesia.

conditions are so difficult and most birds are rare. But exactly for that reason, you can walk the same forest trails over and over again and still find species you have not seen before, especially early in the morning and if you can recognize each bird's call. It seems that the more you learn about the rainforest the more you discover there is to find out. Many resident birds in this region have not been properly studied and their nests have never been found.

With reference to habitat, primary forest is used in this book to indicate primeval, un-logged growth, that is mainly accessible in national parks; secondary/ logged/disturbed forest forms the forest reserves and regrown areas that have often been left for many years. Such areas can be good for birds, especially if there is primary forest nearby.

At higher elevations, that is over 600 metres above sea level and especially above 900 metres, the rainforest and the associated bird life changes its composition altogether. In Peninsular Malaysia alone, there are no less than 66 resident forest species that you will never see below 900 metres. Hence, going up to one of the hill stations in that region is for the birdwatcher like travelling to a new continent.

However, even the tropical rainforest is not uniform. Vast expanses of swamp forest on Borneo, for example, appear lush and green, but the giant trees grow on soil of low fertility, have few fruiting varieties among them and are in fact relatively poor for birds. For the birdwatcher it pays to do his or her homework and to study the books recommended on pages 101, 102, 105, 107 and 108, before travelling to the best places.

As mentioned previously, as the climate changes so do the birds. In eastern Indonesia, the landscape becomes drier, the vegetation lower and less dense, and different birds are seen. In northern Thailand, the edge of the tropical area is encountered, so subtropical species start showing themselves. In parks you will see different species, and bodies of water will attract different ones again. It is this variety that makes birdwatching so fascinating.

Species Covered
During the northern winter months, migrants from northern Asia start appearing, especially along the coasts. Some are numerous and regular visitors, others are rare vagrants that have simply lost their way during their migration. These rare stragglers might be exciting to spot, but most will come from

Above: Pink-necked Green Pigeon (Treron vernans).

a breeding area where they are common. Of special interest in the Oriental region are the birds that cannot be seen anywhere else. The selection in this book therefore concentrates on showing resident Oriental region birds that do not occur outside the region. More than 1,500 species can be found in South-east Asia, so although they cannot all be shown here, representatives from most of the families and especially all the typical Oriental resident families are covered.

Threatened Species

These days the plight of endemic and threatened birds is being given special attention by researchers and decision-makers in an attempt to conserve the world's biodiversity. For the casual birdwatcher, coming across one such bird is also a special moment. In this book, birds occurring within only one national state (national endemics) or one island (island endemics) are featured; in other studies, birds found within an area of 50,000 square kilometres or less are also labelled endemics or restricted-range species.

Above: Chinese Egret (Egretta eulophotes).

When defining threatened birds, the ground-breaking work by N.J. Collar, M.J. Crosby and A.J. Stattersfield, *Birds to Watch 2, The World List of Threatened Birds*, BirdLife International, 1994, has been used for reference. The country listings have on some occasions been criticized by local scholars as either too long or not long enough but have been used here on the basis that they provide some indication of status until a revision has been made. Ambitious projects are at the moment in progress identifying all the threatened birds and all the important bird areas in Asia. With help, BirdLife International will soon be able to provide clear information on the status of all the birds of the region. There are great opportunities for those who

want to involve themselves in studies or conservation of the birds of South-east Asia.

A Word on Nomenclature

For the novice birdwatcher, the challenge of finding and identifying different birds can become easier if some familiarity is made with the taxonomic system that categorizes birds. The taxonomic class, Birds, is divided into orders, then families, genera and finally species. There are also suborders, subfamilies and subspecies, but this book only deals with two levels: species and families, with occasional reference to genera. Since the first part of a bird's two-part Latin name indicates its genus, these names can be quite helpful.

When birds are listed taxonomically, a conventional system is followed beginning with the oldest families, the waterbirds and the seabirds, and moving through all the families to finish with the most advanced families belonging to the order of perching birds, Passeriformes. The subject is fascinating and well worth a thorough study; for further information, see some of the works mentioned in the back of this book.

It is not unusual for scientists to disagree on how to classify birds, and today there is much controversy over how to name and group Asian birds. The conventional system is being challenged by a new method based on DNA-hybridization that was first introduced by Sibley and Monroe in 1990. This system was adopted by the Oriental Bird Club in their annotated checklist of 1996, but it has yet to be adopted in field guides. Since the illustrated field identification guide is the 'bible' of the birdwatcher, the new classification and its associated names will not be in common use until the guide books have all been updated, which could take many years. Therefore, the 'old' names of species and families have been used as in B. King *et al.* (1975), with some updated revisions as in Lekagul & Round (1991) and MacKinnon & Phillipps (1993); at present, these are the three major field guides for South-east Asia (*see* pages 101 and following).

Below: Crimson Sunbird (Aethopyga siparaja) male.

The Case for Photographs

Guide books used for identifying birds in the field are best based on drawings or paintings. The artist does his or her work while looking at the birds from a distance in the field or studies dead birds' skins kept in museums to get all the features and dimensions exactly right. Even the rarest and shyest birds can be illustrated in this way.

However, nothing can capture a bird quite like a photograph. That is why I feel that there is an important niche for photography in wildlife documentation. A good photograph of a bird should show it in its typical pose, in perfect plumage and should include a portion of the habitat in which it prefers to rest, feed and live. In this way it tells a small story about the bird and its way of life, and that is the reason why a bird should preferably be photographed in the wild; showing it in an artificial captive environment really defeats the whole object of the exercise. Today, birds from other regions are rarely pictured in captivity; Asian birds shouldn't be either.

Some birds are very difficult to photograph in the field, for example pheasants and some babblers, pittas and other elusive rainforest species. But as more and more talented wildlife photographers start to work in Asia, more splendid photographs become available. I am proud to say that for the first time in a book on South-east Asian birds, all the birds are shown in their natural environment, moving freely about without any constraints or manipulation – the way birds should live and be enjoyed.

Above: Rufous-necked Hornbill (Aceros nipalensis) male.

Streaked Weaver (Ploceus manyar) male.

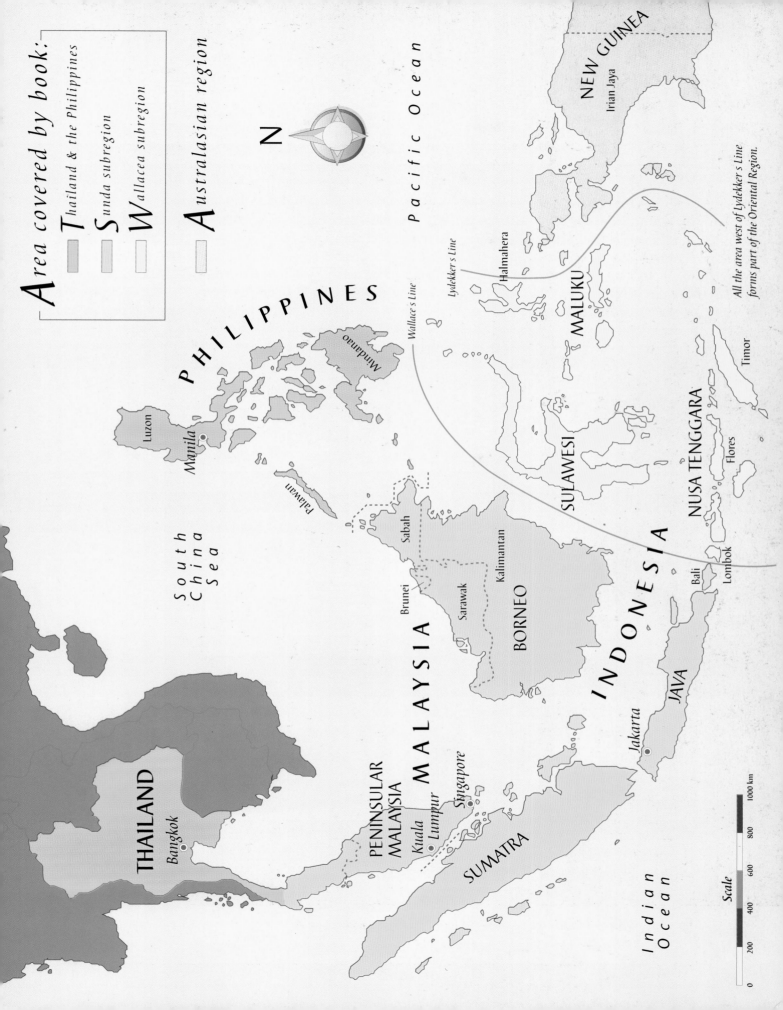

HERONS

THROUGHOUT SOUTH-EAST ASIA *the herons (Ardeidae) are conspicuous birds in the landscape. The herons, night-herons, white egrets and bitterns are all part of this family. All herons live near water, although the Cattle Egret especially can also be seen on open grassy fields in drier areas. They all feed on fish and other aquatic prey which they catch with their strong beaks. Some of the larger species and the egrets are quite adaptable and can live near cultivated areas and flooded paddy-fields. They can be seen walking slowly at the edge of vegetation or flying across swamps or seashore. Other herons, like bitterns and night-herons, are shy, elusive and difficult to see well. They tend to spend most of their lives in dense freshwater vegetation near the banks of rivers, lakes and reservoirs. Many of the species are migratory, with the result that during the northern winter months there tend to be even more herons in the tropics. The various heron species are usually fairly easy to tell apart – except the white egrets where several species are confusingly similar.*

In winter plumage, the JAVAN POND-HERON (Ardeola speciosa) is similar to the CHINESE POND-HERON (A. bacchus), which is a common winter visitor in the region, coming from China as its name indicates. However, during the breeding season it is strikingly different with chestnut-brown neck and breast. Quite a shy bird, the Javan Pond-Heron occurs only in South-east Asia within a patchy range covering parts of Indonesia, Malaysia, Thailand and Indochina; locally it can be numerous around wetlands like marshes, wet paddy-fields and mangroves. The snow-white wings make the bird appear much paler as soon as it takes off.

Left: Possibly the most numerous of all the herons in the region, the LITTLE HERON (*Butorides striatus*) can be seen at both freshwater wetlands and coastal mudflats and mangroves, and sometimes even on exposed rocky shorelines and concrete embankments. During the winter, the resident populations are augmented by migrants from further north in Asia.

Right: The YELLOW BITTERN (*Ixobrychus sinensis*) is resident in most of South-east Asia, but migrants from China and Japan reach eastern Indonesia. It mostly lives secretly in dense vegetation around freshwater swamps, but also occurs at the edges of saline mangrove coasts.

Above: The PURPLE HERON (*Ardea purpurea*) is a common and fairly conspicuous bird throughout most of South-east Asia. It walks at the edge of the reeds along marshes and streams in search of aquatic prey. During the breeding season it nests in colonies in trees near fresh water.

Right: The GREAT EGRET (*Egretta alba*) has a nearly worldwide distribution and occurs throughout the region. It is the biggest and heaviest of the white egrets and is easy to spot when it moves about in open wetlands, of both fresh- and saltwater, on the lookout for fish.

WATERBIRDS

THERE ARE FEW *ducks and other waterfowl in tropical South-east Asia compared with adjacent regions like India and Australia. There is simply not much suitable habitat available and what there is tends to be less productive for waterfowl. Among the ducks (Anatidae) only the treeducks, or whistling-ducks as they are also called because of their ringing calls, are really numerous residents.*

Above: Unlike herons, storks (Ciconiidae) are rare in South-east Asia. The MILKY STORK (Mycteria cinerea) is a globally threatened stork that depends on mangrove forests for nesting sites. It feeds on mudskippers (small fish) which are abundant, but it does not adapt well to human disturbance. In this region, it can be found only along the west coast of Peninsular Malaysia and in parts of Indonesia, notably Sumatra and Java.

Left: Unlike its rarer relatives, the ASIAN OPENBILL (Anastomus oscitans) is locally quite common in Thailand. At Wat Phai Lom north of Bangkok there is a large colony of 8,000—12,000 breeding pairs that can be observed during the dry season under almost zoo-like conditions. This stork lives mainly on snails that it extracts from their shells with its peculiar bill.

Above: The LESSER TREEDUCK *(Dendrocygna javanica) is common in marshes, lakes and reservoirs throughout most of the region. In Eastern Indonesia and the Philippines, the closely related* WANDERING TREEDUCK *(D. arcuata)* (left) *takes over. The treeducks feed on water plants and nest in hollow trees or sometimes in tall grasses or reeds.*

Right: The LESSER ADJUTANT *(Leptoptilos javanicus) is a rare stork that occurs in a patchy range throughout Thailand, Malaysia and parts of Indonesia. It prefers muddy seashores and mangroves, but is nowhere common and is listed as vulnerable to extinction by BirdLife International. This individual is flying across a backdrop of the Bali Barat National Park in west Bali.*

BIRDS OF PREY

HAWKS (ACCIPITRIDAE) ARE *the main family of the group. It is a large family that includes kites, harriers, vultures, buzzards and eagles. The family is varied and diverse, and in Thailand alone there are 43 different species. Some of the smaller sparrowhawks can be difficult to tell apart in the field, but otherwise most species have distinctive features.*

Above: The RUFOUS-BELLIED EAGLE (*Hieraaetus kienerii*) *is widespread throughout the South-east Asia region where large tracts of forest remain, but it is not common anywhere. Little is known about its habits and it is always an exciting bird to spot.*

Right: Widespread throughout the region and throughout the whole of the Oriental and Australasian regions the BRAHMINY KITE (Haliastur indus) *is probably the most conspicuous of the hawks. It prefers open countryside and coastal areas where it can often be seen scavenging on floating food scraps. It is a mystery why this bird is so common in Singapore, where it can even be seen soaring over the city centre, when it is so scarce in nearby Jakarta and has practically disappeared from the whole of Java.*

Right: Most widespread and common of the forest hawks in South-east Asia, the CRESTED SERPENT-EAGLE (Spilornis cheela) *is unmistakable as it sits passively for long periods of time looking out for prey below — which mainly consists of snakes, as the name indicates, plus some mammals and birds as well. Although a forest bird, it prefers more open parts of the rainforest and is also found near clearings, in secondary growth and in mangroves.*

Right: The BLACK KITE (*Milvus migrans*) is a resident and common migrant in the northern part of the region, but it is not so common in the Philippines and Indonesia. Like the Brahminy Kite (*Haliaster indus*), it prefers coastal areas and wetlands, but it can be recognized by its darker plumage and a slightly forked tail (when not widely fanned as here).

Left: King of the sea coasts, the majestic WHITE-BELLIED SEA-EAGLE (*Haliaeetus leucogaster*) can be seen soaring over coastal areas throughout South-east Asia. However, it has declined in numbers over most of its range and is less common now than it once was. It occurs over both muddy mangrove coastlines and along sandy and rocky shores, and can sometimes be seen at rivers and lakes some distance from the sea. It builds its nest in a huge tree or on a remote cliff. It is able to catch fish, but only from the water surface; it does not dive in like an Osprey, and it also feeds on a variety of other prey and scavenges.

Right: The falconets (*Microhierax*) are a charming genus within the falcon family (Falconidae) of very small birds of prey. These raptors are only the size of a starling, or smaller, and feed on cicadas, butterflies, dragonflies and other large insects, and occasionally also small lizards and birds. Although forest birds, the falconets are often seen along forest edges and disturbed patches near primary forest. Four species occur in South-east Asia. This is a COLLARED FALCONET (*M. caerulescens*) from central Thailand.

PHEASANTS

THE PHEASANTS (PHASIANIDAE) *have their stronghold in the Oriental region and there are many species to be found in South-east Asia which is also the eastern limit of their distribution. Pheasants do not occur east of Borneo, and in eastern Indonesia and the Australasian region their biological niche is taken over by the megapodes.*

Pheasants are terrestrial forest birds that seldom fly, preferring to run into thick cover when disturbed. Most species adapt poorly to forest disturbance and many species are threatened with global extinction. Although the males especially are exquisitely plumed, pheasants are notoriously difficult to see in the wild, and even more difficult to photograph. If you spend enough time in the forests of the region you are bound to come across some species, and if you learn their calls you can locate many more, as these are generally loud and diagnostic.

Below: The RED JUNGLEFOWL *(Gallus gallus) is the most numerous bird in the world. Through domestication and selective breeding it has taken on a number of different forms collectively better known as 'the chicken'! The Red Junglefowl still occurs throughout its range which includes South-east Asia, Indochina and other parts of south Asia. Although a forest bird, it is an opportunistic species which also occurs in disturbed forests, and it is omnivorous which probably accounts for its success. This male came out briefly on a forest track in western Thailand, probably attracted by the elephant dung on the road.*

Ong Kiem Sian

Above: Restricted in range to parts of Indochina and Thailand, the beautiful SIAMESE FIREBACK *(Lophura diardi) is listed as vulnerable to extinction, but it can still be seen regularly at the Khao Yai National Park, where this male was photographed.*

Right: The GREEN PEAFOWL (*Pavo muticus*) *is different from the better known Indian Peafowl (P. cristatus) which is a popular captive species. Unlike its south Asian relative, the Green Peafowl is regarded as vulnerable to extinction. It has a peculiar patchy distribution and occurs in South-east Asia only in parts of northern Thailand but not in the rest of the region except for Java, where it is a regular at the Ujung Kulon (east Java) and Baluran (west Java) National Parks. These locations seem to satisfy its habitat preference for open forests and savanna woodlands.*

Below: Also vulnerable to extinction, the CRESTED FIREBACK (*Lophura ignita*) *is endemic to Sunda; its range extends into parts of southern Thailand. It can be seen quite regularly near the Taman Negara Park Headquarters at Kuala Tahan in Malaysia where this photograph of a male was taken.*

Below: The secretive and enigmatic BLACK WOOD-PARTRIDGE (*Melanoperdix nigra*) *is endemic to Sunda and occurs only in Peninsular Malaysia and parts of Sumatra and Borneo. Here it lives on the forest floor of primary lowland rainforest. Little is known of its movements and feeding habits. This rare photograph shows a female at her nest; the male is all black.*

Left: The megapodes or scrubfowl (Megapodiidae) take over from the pheasants as ground-dwelling forest birds east of the Oriental region. They are renowned for their remarkable nesting habits: the eggs are laid in the ground or in a pile of rotting leaves and kept warm by natural heat. East Malaysia has one species that is shared with the Philippines; Indonesia has 14 species. This is a pair of DUSKY SCRUBFOWL (*Megapodius freycinet*) *running through a patch of rainforest on the island of Halmahera in eastern Indonesia.*

RAILS

RAILS (RALLIDAE) ARE *waterbirds with strong legs. They prefer to run into cover when disturbed, but most species are actually migratory and capable of long flights. They tend to be shy and secretive although some species are quite common and easy to see. Many rails are partly nocturnal and can best be observed at dusk and dawn.*

Above: Unmistakable by its large size and turquoise plumage, the PURPLE SWAMPHEN (*Porphyrio porphyrio*) is a resident throughout South-east Asia, but only in more remote low-lying areas where there are large expanses of lakes and marshes. It can often be seen walking in small flocks on the floating vegetation.

Right: BAILLON'S CRAKE (*Porzana pusilla*) is a tiny rail with a wide distribution including most of South-east Asia, where it occurs both as a resident and as a common winter visitor. Very secretive, it rarely flies and can only be seen when it briefly emerges from dense reed vegetation in marshes or beside ponds and lakes.

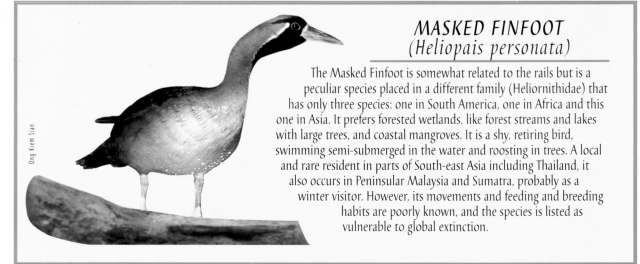

Ong Kiem Sian

MASKED FINFOOT
(*Heliopais personata*)

The Masked Finfoot is somewhat related to the rails but is a peculiar species placed in a different family (Heliornithidae) that has only three species: one in South America, one in Africa and this one in Asia. It prefers forested wetlands, like forest streams and lakes with large trees, and coastal mangroves. It is a shy, retiring bird, swimming semi-submerged in the water and roosting in trees. A local and rare resident in parts of South-east Asia including Thailand, it also occurs in Peninsular Malaysia and Sumatra, probably as a winter visitor. However, its movements and feeding and breeding habits are poorly known, and the species is listed as vulnerable to global extinction.

Right: Found throughout the Oriental region, the
WHITE-BREASTED WATERHEN *(Amaurornis phoenicurus)*
is one of the most delightful birds in South-east Asia. It
occurs in all kinds of wetlands from marshes and lakes to
coastal mangroves. It is very adaptable and thrives in
paddy-fields, drainage canals and even parks and gardens.
It never becomes really tame, however, and runs for
cover if disturbed.

Below: Found only in South-east Asia and parts of Indochina,
the RED-LEGGED CRAKE *(Rallina fasciata) is somewhat of a*
mystery. It is not common anywhere and unlike most other rails
it has a preference for forested areas. It is mostly active by night
and during rainy weather; nothing is known about its feeding
habits; its movements are not understood; and its nest has
never been described.

Ong Kiem Sian.

Left: Rails can sometimes be observed when they emerge
from vegetation early in the morning to dry themselves
off. This is an otherwise very elusive SLATY-BREASTED RAIL
(Gallirallus striatus) that is demonstrating this behaviour.
It occurs only in the Oriental region.

SEABIRDS

SEABIRDS ARE NOT *a family of birds in taxonomic terms, but a category of coastal and pelagic species dependent upon the oceans for food and on remote coastlines and offshore islands for nesting places. Most species are widely distributed throughout the tropical seas, but despite this it is alarming that breeding colonies of seabirds in Asia appear to be declining dramatically in numbers as hunters and egg collectors are able to reach even remote breeding sites in fast motorboats.*

Right: Frigatebirds (Frigatidae) are a family of large seabirds that occur throughout tropical seas. They always move in flocks, sometimes fishing for themselves in the surface waters, sometimes chasing and robbing terns of their catch. They travel far and can be seen in offshore and coastal waters all over the region. They seem to be most numerous in Indonesia, where one species also breeds. There are only five members worldwide in this family, three of which occur in South-east Asia. This picture shows a CHRISTMAS FRIGATEBIRD (Fregata andrewsi) which can be seen all over the region but only breeds on Christmas Island, south of Indonesia. It is regarded as vulnerable to extinction.

Alan OwYong

Left: Various migratory seabirds can be spotted on their travels through South-east Asia. This RED PHALAROPE (Phalaropus fulicaria), from the small Phalaropidae family, breeds beside tundra lakes in Arctic Siberia but becomes a pelagic (ocean-living) seabird during the winter season. Flocks congregate in tropical waters; this individual is resting on an Indonesian coral reef far from its breeding ground.

Right: Remarkably, there are no resident gulls in tropical South-east Asia, and only a few species are recorded as rare vagrants. There are, however, plenty of terns, which are treated by some scientists as part of the gull family (Laridae) and by others as their own family (Sternidae). Care is needed to differentiate between some tern species, but the GREAT CRESTED TERN (Sterna bergii) is easily recognized. It is one of the larger species, and like all terns catches fish in the water, sometimes diving in powerfully from a great height. It breeds on remote islets and rocks in the South China Sea, and outside the breeding season it often moves into coastal waters, resting on kelong poles near the shore.

Above: The BLACK-NAPED TERN (Sterna sumatrana) is one of the commonest terns in the region. It breeds on offshore islets in all the South-east Asian countries including Singapore. A gregarious bird, it always moves in flocks, both during and outside the breeding season, sometimes with other terns.

Brenda Holcombe/Windrush Photos

Above: Boobies are part of the gannet family (Sulidae). They are strictly pelagic birds, highly mobile but seldom seen near the coast. They appear to have declined in numbers as their breeding colonies on remote offshore islets in the South China Sea are vulnerable to disturbance. Four boobies occur in the region, three of which, including the MASKED BOOBY (Sula dactylatra) seen here, are resident.

Right: Although not related to gulls, the tropicbirds (Phaethontidae) can superficially look like huge terns with elaborate wing-beats. It is a small family with only three species, two of which breed in remote parts of South-east Asia. A good place to see tropicbirds is Nusa Penida near Bali, where they land on the steep rocky cliffs facing the sea. Otherwise this bird is strictly pelagic and does not usually come near shores. This one is the RED-TAILED TROPICBIRD (Phaethon rubricauda).

Anders Trevad

SHOREBIRDS

THIS IS A collective term for a number of bird families which are all long-legged and long-billed wading birds that usually live near sheltered and shallow sea coasts. The different families are all part of the order, Charadriiformes, which also includes gulls and terns. Most but not all shorebirds are temperate and Arctic birds that occur in South-east Asia as migrants and winter visitors from the north.

David Tipling/Windrush Photos

Above: A member of a small peculiar family (Burhinidae), the BEACH THICK-KNEE (Esacus magnirostris) is sparsely distributed throughout South-east Asia, and southwards into northern Australia. It is not numerous anywhere but you might find one or a pair together on their preferred habitat of remote sandy and rocky shorelines, estuaries and offshore islands. It feeds exclusively on crustaceans which it crushes with its powerful beak.

The stints are sparrow sized, and are the smallest of the sandpipers. The LONG-TOED STINT (Calidris subminuta) (above) is more brownish in appearance than the RUFOUS-NECKED STINT (Calidris ruficollis) (right) which does not show much rufous in winter plumage. To some birdwatchers, wader-watching is fascinating, but others find the many similar species, often viewed at great distances, uninteresting and prefer to visit the forests.

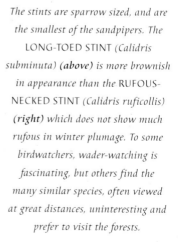

Above: While most shorebirds prefer to congregate on sheltered mudflats, some species choose to feed on exposed, sandy beaches. The SANDERLING (*Calidris alba*) of the sandpiper family and the GREY PLOVER (*Pluvialis squatarola*) are two of them, here seen side by side with the plover on the right. Both are high Arctic birds that breed in a barren tundra landscape.

Above: While sandpipers feed by continuously picking in the mud from side to side as they walk forward, plovers run so fast that they appear to roll across the surface, stopping abruptly to look and poke in the mud for worms. This LITTLE RINGED PLOVER (*Charadrius dubius*) is tapping its right foot in the mud to stir up food.

Right: A MARSH SANDPIPER (*Tringa stagnatilis*) is reflected in the shallow coastal water where it feeds.

Left: The GREATER PAINTED-SNIPE (*Rostratula benghalensis*) is one of the many peculiar birds in the region. Together with a close relative in South America, they are the only members of the family, painted-snipes (*Rostratulidae*). It is widely distributed in South-east Asia but is not common anywhere. It frequents overgrown swamps, but since it is semi-nocturnal and prefers to stay in dense cover it is difficult to see unless flushed. This is a female; unusually, she leaves the nest as soon as she has laid her eggs, leaving the more drab male to stay and rear the young.

Above: A member of the small pratincole family (*Glareolidae*) the ORIENTAL PRATINCOLE (*Glareola maldivarum*) is resident in Thailand and northern Malaysia, and migratory to the rest of the region. It can sometimes be seen in large flocks near other shorebirds. The pratincole prefers open coastal areas and large, dry fields. It is an elegant flyer and feeds on insects which it catches in the air.

Left: Sandpipers (Scolopacidae) make up the largest of the shorebird families. Amazingly in South-east Asia, no member of this family has been confirmed as breeding in the region in spite of so many different species occuring here – in small Singapore alone there are 34 different sandpiper species. The WOOD SANDPIPER (*Tringa glareola*) is one of the most numerous, with flocks visiting both sea coasts and flooded fields further inland.

Plovers (Charadriidae) are another large family of shorebirds. Two of the most common species in the region are the MONGOLIAN PLOVER (*Charadrius mongolus*) *(above)* and the PACIFIC GOLDEN PLOVER (*Pluvialis fulva*) *(left)* which is seen here in front of a flock of CURLEW SANDPIPERS (*Calidris ferruginea*).

PIGEONS

GREEN PIGEONS ARE *chunky, arboreal birds while imperial pigeons are the largest of the group; fruit-doves are smaller, more elegant fruit-eaters while doves tend to come down to the ground and feed on grain. All are members of the same family, Columbidae. All pigeons are strong flyers that can often be seen travelling at high speed across the forest canopy, commuting to and from fruiting trees. Among the green pigeons and some doves the male is more colourful than the female.*

Above: *Locally common in the right habitat throughout much of the region, this* MOUNTAIN IMPERIAL PIGEON *(Ducula badia) is an attractive bird that is often seen at fruiting trees in montane and submontane forests.*

Above: *Like all doves the* PEACEFUL DOVE *(Geopelia striata) likes to come down to the ground to feed, especially in open countryside and cultivated areas and villages. Although native to only South-east Asia, it is a popular cage bird and has established wild populations in far-away places like Madagascar and Hawaii.*

Right: *The* PINK-NECKED PIGEON *(Treron vernans) is one of the most characteristic birds of the region. It only occurs in South-east Asia and Indochina, reaching Sulawesi and the Lesser Sundas or Nusa Tenggara. It is tree-dwelling but not a forest bird, and is most commonly found in secondary growth, mangroves and even parks and gardens in Asian cities, where it can be seen feeding on ornamental fruiting trees right above the traffic. This picture shows a male.*

Right: This pretty RED TURTLE-DOVE (*Streptopelia tranquebarica*) is common throughout Thailand and the Philippines but does not occur in the rest of the region except for Singapore. Here, a large population of escaped birds has settled in semi-developed parts of the republic that resemble this dove's preferred habitat of open countryside and scattered woodlands.

Right: Cuckoo-doves are brown-spotted, forest doves with long tails. This SLENDER-BILLED CUCKOO-DOVE (*Macropygia amboinensis*) occurs from Sulawesi across eastern Indonesia into New Guinea.

Below: A green pigeon, the THICK-BILLED PIGEON (*Treron curvirostra*) is a forest bird. It is common in primary and secondary lowland forest, including mangroves, throughout Southeast Asia, including Sumatra and Borneo, but not further east. This female is feeding in the top of a large fig tree.

PARROTS

THE FAMILY OF PARROTS *(Psittacidae) is, next to the hummingbirds, the largest of all bird families with 271 species worldwide. In South-east Asia the family is not that well represented, but there are many parrots in the adjacent Australasian region. While Malaysia has five parrot species, neighbouring Indonesia has 76, mostly in the eastern part of the country. Parrots vary greatly in size but they are all colourful birds with powerful bills and noisy, screeching calls. They are popular cage birds and many species have declined due to the captive bird trade.*

Right: All parrots feed on vegetable matter that they crush with their strong beaks. This little RED-FLANKED LORIKEET *(Charmosyna placentis) from eastern Indonesia favours flowering trees.*

Far right: Endemic to the Philippines and some islands near Borneo, the BLUE-NAPED PARROT *(Tanygnathus lucionensis), shown here in this rare photograph, is now very scarce in the wild, mainly due to habitat loss and capture for the bird trade.*

Pete Morris

Below: A male ECLECTUS PARROT *(Eclectus roratus), a large and conspicuous parrot that is distributed throughout eastern Indonesia and southwards to Australia.*

Right: Found in eastern Indonesia, New Guinea and Australia, the RED-CHEEKED PARROT (*Geoffroyus geoffroyi*) is locally common in forests and nearby cultivation. This is a female.

Below: A pretty VIOLET-NECKED LORY (*Eos squamata*) which is endemic to eastern Indonesia.

Right: The LONG-TAILED PARAKEET (*Psittacula longicauda*) has a restricted distribution in Malaysia, Borneo, Sumatra and a few adjacent islands. It does not do well in captivity, but in the wild it is an adaptable species found both in forests and in secondary growth, plantations and parks. This female is looking for a new home; all parrots live in cavities in trees. Parrots like to fly about in little groups calling loudly, especially late in the day before they settle to roost.

CUCKOOS

CUCKOOS (CUCULIDAE) FORM *a large family of birds which is well represented in South-east Asia. The genera of so-called true cuckoos are parasitic breeders, that is, they lay their eggs in other birds' nests. Other groups like malkohas and coucals, however, build their own nests and rear their young. All cuckoos feed on insects and caterpillars, the larger species also feeding on frogs and small reptiles.*

Below: Although one of the commonest birds of South-east Asia's open countryside and grasslands, the LESSER COUCAL (Centropus bengalensis) is not easy to view well. It usually stays near the ground in tall grass and makes only short flights low across the vegetation.

Above: Endemic to Sunda like many other malkoha species, the RED-BILLED MALKOHA (Phaenicophaeus javanicus) is not as common as some of its relatives.

Right: The CHESTNUT-BREASTED MALKOHA *(Phaenicophaeus curvirostris) occurs in primary and sometimes secondary lowland forest in the Sunda subregion, extending into southern Philippines. Like other malkohas, you almost always see a pair moving through the forest together.*

Below: One of the smaller cuckoos, the MALAYAN BRONZE CUCKOO *(Chrysococcyx minutillus) is found from southern Thailand through the Malay Peninsula and all of Indonesia, but it is not common anywhere. This is a juvenile that has been fostered by the* FLYEATER *(Gerygone sulphurea) on the right.*

Below: Easily recognized by its very long tail, the GREEN-BILLED MALKOHA *(Phaenicophaeus tristis) prefers a less dense habitat than some of the other malkohas. In Malaysia and Sumatra it is a submontane bird, but in Thailand and further west within the Oriental region it can be found in deciduous woodlands and scrub.*

Above: With an apt name, the GIANT COUCAL *(Centropus goliath), endemic to a few islands in eastern Indonesia, is a massive bird. Although locally common, it is surprisingly difficult to see well, always staying hidden by vegetation and rarely flying.*

NIGHTBIRDS

MANY BIRDS ARE *active by night. Rails, for instance, and many shorebirds will feed at low tide by night, especially if the moon is out. But some families of birds are active only by night, and the three most important ones are mentioned here.*

Left: The frogmouths (Podargidae) are an enigmatic, poorly-known family. All species are forest birds that are difficult to find and observe, and also difficult to distinguish, even by call. Unlike nightjars (Caprimulgidae), which catch flying insects, frogmouths find prey in the trees or on the ground. This is a rare photograph of a PHILIPPINE FROGMOUTH (Batrachostomus septimus) which is endemic to the Philippines.

Pete Morris

Right: The most widespread nightjar is the LARGE-TAILED NIGHTJAR (Caprimulgus macrurus) which can be found in the whole of the Oriental region and all through Indonesia. At night it hunts for insects near forest edges or utters a frog-like call repeatedly; during the day it roosts on a branch. This individual is sitting on its nest, which is just a depression in the bare ground.

Left: The owls (Strigidae) are nocturnal birds of prey with mottled brown plumage and round heads. The COLLARED SCOPS-OWL (Otus lempiji) is distributed throughout South-east Asia, except in eastern Indonesia where similar but separate species occur. It is an adaptable bird living both in forests and disturbed habitats, and even parks and gardens. During the breeding season, its hooting call can be heard on quiet evenings all over the region. This adult is feeding a house gecko to its young.

Overlapping with the Collared Scops-Owl in Thailand, the ORIENTAL SCOPS-OWL *(Otus sunia) has a more northerly and westerly distribution, but migrates outside the breeding season into other parts of the region.*

Uthai Treesucon

SWIFTS

SWIFTS (APODIDAE), AN *elegant family of birds, have aerodynamic bodies and long, narrow, bent wings. They fly with rapid wing-beats interspersed with long glides. Swifts spend more time flying than any other bird, feeding, drinking and even sleeping on the wing. During high-pressure weather they move high; in cloudy weather they come low to the ground. They never perch, and only land when they have to nest, which they do on vertical cliff faces, in buildings or in hollow trees. Some of the smaller species nest in dark caves in which they navigate by an amazing ability to locate by sound.*

Left: The Aerodramus genus of swiftlets is a taxonomic puzzle and a challenge for the field observer; the different species can be very difficult to tell apart in flight. This is a UNIFORM SWIFTLET (A. vanikorensis) from eastern Indonesia, one of the echolocating species.

Right: The swiftlets are the smallest of the swifts and the WHITE-BELLIED SWIFTLET (Collocolia esculenta) is the smallest of the swiftlets, measuring only 9 centimetres, which is less than the smallest sunbird. It is, however, a very successful bird and is found all over the region, feeding in flocks over forests and open countryside at all altitudes.

Above: The small WHISKERED TREESWIFT (Hemiprocne comata) is found in most of South-east Asia and has similar habits to the Grey-rumped Treeswift, but it is more of a rainforest bird than its larger relative. This is a male; note the extremely long wings that extend out over the tail.

Left: *True to its name, the HOUSE SWIFT (Apus affinis) is associated with man throughout its range, which includes all of South-east Asia. Except in the Philippines, it is a common bird in all the countries of the region. It has taken to nesting only on buildings and other artificial structures like towers and bridges. It seems to nest year-round, often returning to the breeding colony to roost. An evening in a South-east Asian city or town just would not be the same without House Swifts flying low overhead, filling the air with their piercing calls.*

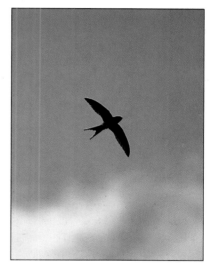

Centre right: The treeswifts are an unusual family (Hemiprocnidae). There are only four members of the family and they all occur in different parts of South-east Asia. The GREY-RUMPED TREESWIFT (Hemiprocne longipennis) is distributed throughout South-east Asia and is a common bird in forested areas, forest edges, and even parks, but it is never numerous or seen in flocks. Unlike other swifts, it perches readily and spends much time in the trees sitting on an exposed top branch flying out for insects, on occasions like a bee-eater. Amazingly, it does not build a nest, but lays its egg directly onto a horizontal branch.

Right: Needletails are large, cigar-shaped swifts. The largest is the BROWN NEEDLETAIL (Hirundapus giganteus), shown here, which is regarded as the fastest bird in the world. It occurs as a resident and a migrant throughout South-east Asia, catching insects over forested regions in the lowlands and the mountains.

TROGONS

TROGONS (TROGONIDAE) ARE *a small family of tropical forest birds found in small numbers throughout South-east Asia except Singapore, where all trogons, like so many other forest birds, are now locally extinct. The Philippines has its own endemic species, otherwise there are none east of Borneo. Trogons are lethargic birds that sit still in the mid-storey of primary forest for long periods at a time and then suddenly vanish from sight. They catch insects in the air but this is rare to see. Memorizing their diagnostic calls will help locate them. Trogons are sexually dimorphic; the males always have brighter colours than the females. They nest in cavities in trees, but few nests have been found in this region. Trogons do not do well in captivity, so you are unlikely to find any in the local bird park. It is necessary to get out onto the forest trails to see them.*

Right: The RED-NAPED TROGON *(Harpactes kasumba) has a similar distribution and habitat preference to Diard's Trogon (see below). This is a male.*

Below: DIARD'S TROGON *(Harpactes diardii) is endemic to the Sunda subregion where it can be found in primary and mature secondary rainforest. It is not common anywhere and it is always a bit of a bonus spotting one during a morning's birdwatching. This is a female.*

Above: The RED-HEADED TROGON *(Harpactes erythrocephalus) is a montane and submontane trogon distributed widely from the Himalayas through Thailand and Peninsular Malaysia to Sumatra but not Borneo, which has an endemic montane species. It can be found between 700 and 2,000 metres elevation but it is not common anywhere. This is a male.*

Restricted to the Sunda subregion, the SCARLET-RUMPED TROGON *(Harpactes duvaucelii) occurs in lowland forest and is probably the most likely member of the family to be seen. It is smaller than most other trogons and tends to perch lower down. The female (left) is less brightly coloured than the male (right).*

Uthai Treesucon

KINGFISHERS

KINGFISHERS (ALCEDINIDAE) ARE *colourful birds with strong bills, usually seen perched on low branches or sticks. Some species live near water and dive to catch fish, but in South-east Asia most are open country or forest birds that feed on insects and small reptiles, often far from water. They live singly or in pairs, often staying long in the same territory, and regularly using the same perch; some species migrate. Kingfishers fly in a rapid and direct manner, frequently uttering a harsh and penetrating call as they take off.*

Above: *The BLUE-EARED KINGFISHER (Alcedo meninting) might look superficially like the Common Kingfisher, but its plumage is deeper blue and it lacks the rufous patch behind the eye. Restricted to the Oriental region, it is a shy bird found at streams and ponds in remote forested areas, and lowland rainforest rivers and creeks. Like the Common, it catches fish from a perch and when disturbed flies off low across the water with a piercing trilling call.*

Above: *Endemic to Indonesia, the SMALL BLUE KINGFISHER (Alcedo coerulescens) occurs only on Java and Bali plus nearby Lombok and the southern tip of Sumatra. It can be fairly common locally in the right habitat of shallow coastlines, mangroves and estuaries, where it lives on fish.*

Left: *The COLLARED KINGFISHER (Halcyon chloris) is one of the most common of all kingfishers in South-east Asia, especially along the coast and in mangroves, but also in open woodlands, parks and gardens further inland. It feeds on crabs, insects or lizards that it catches on the ground. A pair is highly territorial, often displaying and calling loudly together. The nest is built either in a mudbank or in a hollow tree. This individual is sunning itself in the early morning light.*

Right: A large kingfisher with a huge bill, the STORK-BILLED KINGFISHER (Halcyon capensis) is widely distributed throughout South-east Asia east to Nusa Tenggara in Indonesia. Locally, for instance on Borneo, it can be fairly common. It frequents both coastal mangroves and large inland rivers, where it can be seen sitting high on a perch looking for fish and crustaceans in the water below.

ORIENTAL DWARF KINGFISHER (Ceyx erithacus)

Only the size of a sparrow, the pretty Oriental Dwarf Kingfisher is one of the most exciting birds of the South-east Asian rainforests. It is an Oriental region species that is sometimes split into two: the BLACK-BACKED KINGFISHER, a migratory race breeding in the northern part of the region and the RUFOUS-BACKED KINGFISHER (C. rufidorsus) seen here, which is an endemic resident of Sunda. While the migratory race strays into disturbed habitats during its travels, the rufous-backed variety can only be found inside primary and mature-secondary lowland forests, often near a small stream. However, it does not seem to catch fish, preferring insects instead. This extremely shy, small jewel of the forest is hard to view well, but is often encountered by chance when it flies rapidly across a forest patch calling with a high-pitched trill.

Above: The BANDED KINGFISHER (*Lacedo pulchella*) *is a peculiar forest bird, restricted in range to South-east Asia, but not really common anywhere. It is not associated with water at all and when seen it usually sits motionless for long periods at a time, mid-storey in the lowland rainforest.*

Above: The WHITE-THROATED KINGFISHER (*Halcyon smyrnensis*) *is a successful bird that enjoys a wide distribution across most of Asia and south into the Malay Peninsula and Sumatra. It frequents open countryside and woodlands, including cultivated areas and parks. Although often seen near water it does not fish but catches insects and lizards in vegetation.*

Right: Most migrants in equatorial South-east Asia come to the region from the great landmasses in northern Asia during the northern winter. THE SACRED KINGFISHER (*Halcyon sanctus*), *however, is one of those few visiting Indonesia from Australia during the southern winter, reaching as far north as Borneo and west to Sumatra. It stays around sea coasts and can be distinguished from the resident Collared Kingfisher by the brownish, not pure white, flanks.*

Left: The COMMON KINGFISHER (Alcedo atthis) has a widespread distribution and is one of the few resident birds in this region that can also be found in Europe, part of the Palaearctic region. It breeds in Thailand, Malaysia and Indonesia but only rarely and locally. It is, however, a very common winter visitor and can be seen during most months of the year, always near water of some kind, be it flowing or stagnant, fresh or salt. It frequents open country and often busy places, like fish ponds, coastal embankments and even city drainage canals. It sits on either a branch, a pole or a rock over the water and plunges in for small fish below.

Above: The BLACK-CAPPED KINGFISHER (Halcyon pileata) breeds in China and Korea, but migrates south during the winter and is then a common visitor to South-east Asia, especially in open countryside, mangroves and on swampy river banks.

BEE-EATERS, ROLLERS AND THE HOOPOE

THESE COLOURFUL BIRDS *form three families. Bee-eaters (Meropidae) are colourful, mainly greenish birds with slender bodies and long bills which they use to snatch insects in the air. Most species are open country birds that perch on dead branches or wires, often in little groups. Sometimes many congregate at breeding colonies or roosting sites during migration. The nest is a burrow in an embankment or on the flat ground. They are vocal birds with soft, chuckling calls.*

Top Left: There are two kinds of bee-eaters; the open country Merops species and the Nyctyornis bee-eaters. This is the RED-BEARDED BEE-EATER (Nyctyornis amictus), which is a chunky, sluggish bird restricted to the Sunda subregion, where it is found only in the rainforest, tall primary forest or mature-secondary growth from the lowlands occasionally up to submontane forest at 1,400 metres. It perches in the mid-storey and canopy levels and appears generally less active than the agile Merops bee-eaters.

Left: Smallest of all the bee-eaters, the GREEN BEE-EATER (Merops orientalis) is one of those Oriental birds that prefers dry subtropical deciduous woodlands. Therefore, in this region it occurs only in Thailand where it is locally very common.

Rollers (Coraciidae) are fairly large, bulky birds that perch in the open, flying out to catch insects in the air or dropping down to the ground for prey, such as large invertebrates and small lizards. The Hoopoe is one of those unique birds that forms its own family (Upupidae).

Left: The INDIAN ROLLER (Coracias benghalensis), with its iridescent blue wings, is a widespread roller that does not penetrate the humid tropics. In South-east Asia it reaches northern Peninsular Malaysia; further north in Thailand it is, however, very common in dry, open country and cultivated areas.

Below: The DOLLARBIRD (Eurystomus orientalis), a member of the Roller family, is named for the white patch on the wing visible in flight which presumably resembles an American silver dollar. It is a widespread Asian bird and is common in all South-east Asian countries. Although never numerous, two birds are usually seen together. The nest is built in a tree cavity, often in a dead coconut tree.

Above: The HOOPOE (Upupa epops) has a wide distribution throughout Asia, Europe and Africa. In South-east Asia, only Thailand offers the right habitat of dry woodlands and cultivated areas that it prefers, and it is only a rare vagrant to other parts of the region.

HORNBILLS

THE FAMILY OF HORNBILLS *(Bucerotidae)* has perhaps captured the imagination of visitors to the rainforest more than any other family of birds. Seeing one or more hornbills fly across the forest canopy is the highlight of any birdwatching trip in South-east Asia. Maybe it is simply because hornbills are so big and peculiar looking, or maybe it is because they are quite easy to observe. They fly far every day in search of fruiting trees and when they find a large tree with ripe figs they gather together, often with two or three species represented in the same tree. It is a truly spectacular sight. Outside the breeding season, species such as the Wreathed Hornbill *(Rhyticeros undulatus)* gather in flocks of sometimes hundreds of individuals which fly and roost together.

Hornbills are true rainforest birds; apart from one species, the Oriental Pied Hornbill, all 20 South-east Asian hornbills depend on primary rainforest for nesting. Therefore if you see hornbills you know that you are in a virgin forest, or at least that one is nearby.

Above: The ORIENTAL PIED HORNBILL *(Anthracoceros albirostris), split by some specialists into a southern and a northern species, is the only one of the hornbills in South-east Asia that habitually lives outside primary rainforest. It can often be found in mature secondary forest, forest edges along rivers and coastal forests. Like all hornbills, however, it needs a large living hardwood tree for nesting. This pair has come out to wash in the early morning dew on the foliage and are drying themselves; the male is on the right.*

NESTING HORNBILLS

More than anything else, it is possibly the bizarre nesting habits of hornbills that make them special. At the start of the nesting period the male helps the female seal herself inside a cavity in a live hardwood tree. She stays here at least until the egg has hatched. Some species remain until the nestling is ready to fly off with the female — in total a period of up to 90 days! During this time the male brings the female food and passes it to her through a narrow crack left open in the trunk.

A rare nesting sequence from a nest site of the RHINOCEROS HORNBILL *(Buceros rhinoceros), a species endemic to Sunda.*

Above: *The male flies in with food*

Right: *... regurgitates a fig ...*

Below: *... feeds it to the female inside ...*

Bottom right: *... and takes off again.*

Adisak Vidhidharm

Above: Listed as near-threatened with extinction, this
HELMETED HORNBILL *(Rhinoplax vigil) is found only in
the Sunda subregion and is not common anywhere. It is the only
one of the hornbills that has a massive, ivory-like casque,
and this has been used by locals for handicrafts. Like all
hornbills it is vocal, calling with loud, accelerating laughter,
often just before it takes to the air. This is a rare
photograph of a male near the nesting hole.*

Right: The BLACK HORNBILL *(Anthracoceros malayanus) is a
fairly small species that is endemic to the Sunda subregion
where it is uncommon. It is a resident of the lowland rainforest,
and unlike many other species its range does not extend up into
submontane habitat. This is a male.*

Left: Clearance of the lowland rainforests for development has resulted in a decrease in hornbill numbers. This species, the WRINKLED HORNBILL (*Rhyticeros corrugatus*), has been particularly affected. It is now believed to be extinct in Thailand and is very rarely observed within the rest of its narrow range which includes Malaysia, Borneo and Sumatra. It is regarded as vulnerable to global extinction. A male is shown here.

Left: Generally hornbills are fruit-eaters and congregate in tall, fruiting trees. They also take some animal prey, however, and this BUSHY-CRESTED HORNBILL (*Anorrhinus galeritus*) male is holding a centipede. An endemic to Sunda, this hornbill is atypical as it is not a canopy bird, preferring instead to move below and in between the treetops, never flying high above the forest like other species.

Above: BLYTH'S HORNBILL (*Phyticeros plicatus*) is distributed from Maluku in Indonesia eastward to the island of New Guinea. It is less shy than other hornbills and is quite approachable. This is a pair, with the male on the left.

BARBETS

BARBETS (MEGALAIMIDAE) ARE *small to medium-sized birds with chunky bodies and strong bills. The plumage is mostly green with diagnostic head-patterns of bright red, yellow and blue. All barbets are tree-dwellers and most are forest birds living in primary or secondary rainforest where they visit fruiting trees and nest in tree cavities. They are well represented in South-east Asia but as a typical Oriental region family, no barbets occur east of Wallace's Line. Barbets stay in the canopy or upper storey of the forest, often hidden by foliage, so good views are usually difficult to obtain. Sometimes they will emerge flying with rapid wing beats in a direct manner to the next tree. Their repetitious, hooting calls are diagnostic and aid identification.*

Right: The LINEATED BARBET (Megalaima lineata) is one of those birds of the Oriental region that shies away from the tall, dense and humid forests of the Sunda subregion. It is locally common in Thailand and on Java and Bali where it can find its preferred habitat of dry woodlands and open, coastal forest.

Above: All barbets are green — except the BROWN BARBET (Calorhamphus fuliginosus) which is endemic to Sunda and is treated in a genus of its own. Locally it can be quite a regular bird in primary lowland rainforest, always moving about in small groups and coming out into the open more often than other barbets.

Above: The BLACK-BROWED BARBET (Megalaima oorti) is locally common in montane and submontane forests in Peninsular Malaysia and Sumatra. For some reason it is not found in Thailand, although it also occurs in southern China and Indochina. A small green barbet, it is difficult to see in the trees, but its rhythmic three-note slurring call rings out perpetually over hill stations in areas in which it lives.

Above: The RED-CROWNED BARBET (*Megalaima rafflesii*) is an endemic to Sunda: rare in southern Thailand but locally common in the rest of the subregion where it can be found in primary and sometimes secondary lowland forest. In Singapore, it is the only one of the forest barbets still maintaining a population, four other species having become locally extinct.

Right: The BLUE-EARED BARBET (*Megalaima australis*) is widespread throughout the Oriental region including South-east Asia in primary rainforests, forest edges and secondary growth. It is, however, surprisingly rare to get good views as this small bird stays at canopy level feeding out of sight in dense fruiting trees.

Ong Kiem Sian

Left: The COPPERSMITH BARBET (*Megalaima haemacephala*) is the smallest but also the most successful of the barbets in Asia, probably because it is very adaptable. Originally a mangrove and forest edge bird, it can also be found in disturbed woodlands, plantations and even city parks and gardens. It is fairly common in those habitats throughout South-east Asia, including the Philippines where it is the only member of its family. It calls monotonously with a rapid series of faint hoots, presumably sounding like a coppersmith's hammer.

WOODPECKERS

WOODPECKERS ARE A *large and well-known family (Picidae) that is well represented in the Oriental region: Thailand has 36 species, Malaysia has 24, but the Philippines has only six and Indonesia east of Sulawesi none at all since the family does not extend into the Australasian region. Varying greatly in size and colour, all woodpeckers cling to tree trunks, feed on insect larvae and ants, and nest in dead or living trees in cavities that they excavate themselves with a powerful chipping action of their beaks. Most species have harsh abrupt calls that can aid in identification. Many forest birds use an undulating flight where they intermittently flap and then fold their wings, but the woodpeckers rest so long between flaps that they drop down in characteristically deep curves as they move across the forest.*

Above: The piculets are a peculiar type of diminutive woodpecker. This species, the SPECKLED PICULET *(Picumnus innominatus), is found in montane and submontane forest in Thailand, Peninsular Malaysia, Sumatra and possibly Borneo. Locally it is quite common in mixed forests and bamboo. It is an active bird, hopping along thin branches, and at 10cm in length it is one of the smallest in the region, being only the size of a flowerpecker.*

Right: The BANDED WOODPECKER *(Picus miniaceus) is endemic to the Sunda subregion and is locally common throughout the area, including Singapore. It is found in both primary and secondary rainforest, and forest edges. This is a female inspecting a possible new home.*

Above: The COMMON GOLDENBACK *(Dinopium javanense) is widely distributed throughout the Oriental region and South-east Asia including the Philippines. It is locally common in open woodlands and coastal mangroves. All woodpeckers are sexually dimorphic with the male usually having some red facial pattern as this photograph shows.*

Left: The GREATER YELLOWNAPE (*Picus flavinucha*) has a similar habitat preference and distribution to its lesser relative, and is a good example of how similar species can still find distinct niches in the complex ecosystem of the rainforest.

Below: The LESSER YELLOWNAPE (*Picus chlorolophus*) is locally quite common in submontane forests of the Oriental region including Thailand, Peninsular Malaysia and Sumatra. It often follows the waves of mixed-species flocks that move through the forest feeding together on insects.

Right: The BUFF-RUMPED WOODPECKER (*Meiglyptes tristis*) is another species endemic to Sunda. It is locally common in primary and secondary forest, where it feeds on ants, often down on the lower branches and in scrub, sometimes perching across the branch like a passerine. This is a male.

BROADBILLS

BROADBILLS (EUYLAIMIDAE) ARE *a small family of forest birds typical of South-east Asia. There are only 14 species in the world, of which one is endemic to the Philippines, nine others occur in the Sunda subregion, and seven of these also occur in Thailand. There are no broadbills east of Wallace's Line and the five species that used to live in Singapore are now locally extinct. Broadbills are thickset birds that live on fruits, or insects caught on the wing. They perch in the mid-storey and canopy levels of the forest. Although most species have pretty, delicate colours, the plumage is often difficult to see well in the poor light beneath the dense vegetation in which broadbills live and they are usually located and identified by their calls.*

Below: Many broadbills are for some reason attracted to water — usually swampy patches or streams in the primary forest; the BLACK-AND-RED BROADBILL (Cymbirhynchus macrorhynchos) is attracted more than any other species. Less of a forest bird than other species, this broadbill can be found at river edges and coastal mangrove forests. It also moves lower to the ground than true forest broadbills. Now rare in southern Thailand, it is still locally a common bird in other parts of the Sunda subregion

Uthai Treesucon

Above: Several broadbills have a green plumage with black face patterns. The aptly named GREEN BROADBILL (Calyptomena viridis) is locally fairly common in the lowland forests of the Sunda subregion, but moving at mid-storey and canopy level it is not an easy bird to spot. This is a male.

Right: The BANDED BROADBILL (Eurylaimus javanicus) can be found in primary lowland forest and sometimes disturbed forest from Thailand down through the Sunda subregion. It is nowhere common and has been little studied. Known to hawk for insects in the air, it is a shy bird, usually seen sitting lethargically at upper- to mid-storey levels of the forest as this rare photograph shows.

Alan Ow Yong

Left: *The* DUSKY BROADBILL (*Corydon sumatranus*) *is a lowland forest bird that is widespread in South-east Asia, including Thailand, Malaysia, Sumatra and Borneo, but is not really common anywhere. It is easier to see than some of the other species in the family as it moves in small groups, often making a noise with shrill rising and falling calls. It flies heavily within the forest, just below the canopy.*

Right: *Like all broadbills, the Dusky Broadbill builds a hanging pouch-type nest. However, there are few nesting records of this poorly studied bird. Note how this elaborately constructed nest is suspended from a single thin string of vine.*

Above: *The* MALAYSIAN HONEYGUIDE (*Indicator archipelagicus*) *is part of the honeyguide family (Indicatoridae) named after an African species that leads mammals and humans to bee-hives. This species, however, does not behave in that way and very little is known about it in general. It occurs within the Sunda subregion in primary and secondary rainforest, where it feeds on bees and beeswax, but it is very rare everywhere and its nest has never been found. It has been suggested that it is a nesting parasite on the Brown Barbet. This rare photograph shows an individual perched at mid-storey in the forest of Danum Valley in Sabah, Malaysia.*

Above: *Broadbills do indeed have broad bills; this is a* BLACK-AND-YELLOW BROADBILL (*Eurylaimus ochromalus*), *which at 17 centimetres is smaller than a starling and is the baby of the family. It is endemic to Sunda and is locally common in its habitat of primary or mature-secondary lowland rainforest. It is difficult to view well, as it stays hidden by the foliage of large trees. This picture was taken from a canopy tree-tower, 30 metres off the ground.*

PITTAS

PITTAS (PITTIDAE) ARE *one of the rich rewards when birdwatching in South-east Asia. Some keen birdwatchers have lived in the region for years and never seen a single pitta, others travel in to spend a few weeks or months there and see a handful of different species. What makes pittas so exclusive is the fact that they are hard to find, hard to see and spectacular to look at once you spot them. They are an odd family of forest birds that move on the ground or on low branches. Some are sedentary in primary forest while other species migrate and can then be seen in disturbed habitats. Like pheasants and other ground-dwelling birds, pittas adapt poorly to logged forests where the lower vegetation is generally too dense for them. South-east Asia is the centre for the pitta family and of the world's 29 species no less than 22 can be found in the countries covered in this book.*

Pete Morris

Left: The HOODED PITTA *(Pitta sordida) is a fairly widespread Oriental region species. It is resident in parts of Thailand and the Philippines and a migrant visitor further south in South-east Asia. It hops on the ground in primary forest and, during migration, forest edges and disturbed areas. It probes the ground and turns over dead leaves to grab worms and other invertebrate prey.*

Pete Morris

Above: The BLUE-HEADED PITTA *(Pitta baudii) is endemic to primary lowland rainforest in Borneo. The Danum Valley Field Centre is a regular place to see this rare bird, listed as near-threatened with extinction by BirdLife International.*

Left: The GARNET PITTA *(Pitta granatina) is a dazzling bird, endemic to the Sunda subregion, where the lucky observer will see it in primary forest, often near wet areas, hopping around on the floor or up onto roots and fallen logs.*

Frank Lambert

Uthai Treesucon

Left: The BANDED PITTA (*Pitta guajana*) is a stunning bird but it is frustratingly difficult to find. It is restricted to the Sunda subregion where it lives in primary or mature secondary lowland forest. In the right place you might see it jump across the forest trail but you are more likely only to hear its loud call coming from the ground somewhere. All pittas have diagnostic calls and listening for them is often the only way of locating the birds. This is a male at its nest.

Right: The MANGROVE PITTA (*Pitta megarhyncha*) is near-threatened with extinction as its habitat is disappearing rapidly. It has a small distribution including only parts of southern Thailand, Peninsular Malaysia, Singapore and Sumatra, where it is exclusively a mangrove bird. It can be distinguished from the similar and more widespread Blue-winged Pitta (*P. moluccensis*) by its stronger bill and paler crown feathers.

Below: The stunning AZURE-BREASTED PITTA (*Pitta steerii*) in this rare photograph is endemic to the Philippines and is unfortunately very difficult to see. It is rare everywhere, adapts poorly to disturbance and its habitat is being rapidly destroyed.

Alan Ow Yong

Pete Morris

Right: The lowland rainforest near Krabi in southern Thailand is home to GURNEY'S PITTA (*Pitta gurneyi*), which is found only here and possibly at some unsurveyed sites in nearby Peninsular Myanmar. Gurney's Pitta is one of the rarest birds in the world and is listed as in critical danger of extinction. This rare photograph shows a male at one of the few nests that have been discovered for this species.

Uthai Treesucon

CUCKOO-SHRIKES

CUCKOO-SHRIKES AND MINIVETS *form a common family (Campephagidae). They are arboreal birds, with some living in closed forest and others in open woodlands. None of the cuckoo-shrikes have anything to do with either cuckoos or shrikes, the term is just an attempt to describe these medium-sized, ordinary-looking perching birds, which may in fact be closely related to orioles and crows. Minivets are colourful birds with slender bodies and long tails, the male usually predominantly red, the female yellow. The family is well represented in South-east Asia including eastern Indonesia.*

Above: The minivets are lively and pretty birds that move through the forest canopy in small flocks. They flutter about, always on the move, dashing from tree to tree or resting only briefly in the thin top branches. They keep in contact with high-pitched ringing calls. Several species are similar in appearance; shown here is a male SCARLET MINIVET (Pericrocotus flammeus), an Oriental region bird that is locally common in primary lowland forest.

Below: The MOLUCCAN CUCKOO-SHRIKE (Coracina atriceps) is endemic to islands in the Maluku province of eastern Indonesia, where locally it can be a fairly common bird in forests and mangroves. This individual came down briefly from its high perch to grab an insect off the ground.

Above: There are 47 members of this family in Indonesia, most of which are either endemic to that country, like this RUFOUS-BELLIED TRILLER (Lalage aurea), or spread into the Australasian region only.

Below: The COMMON CICADABIRD *(Coracina tenuirostris) is one of those birds with eastern affinities that extends from Australia into the Wallacea transitional subregion in eastern Indonesia where it is locally common in wooded areas from the lowlands up to submontane hills. It cannot be found in the Oriental region. This is a female.*

SWALLOWS AND MARTINS (Hirundinidae)

Swallows (Hirundinidae) are aerial feeders like swifts but unlike the latter they perch readily on branches and on wires and other man-made structures; they also come down to the ground to drink and collect nesting material. The most common species in South-east Asia is the Pacific Swallow *(Hirundo tahitica)* shown here, which is a common resident in all the countries of the region, especially around open coastal terrain and cultivated areas. The nest is built in buildings, under rooftops, cliff overhangs or under

bridges. During the northern winter this local bird can be confused with the Barn Swallow *(H. rustica)* which has a longer tail and a black breast-band and which comes to the region from temperate Asia in huge numbers.

LEAFBIRDS

IORAS AND LEAFBIRDS *are included in the same family (Chloropseidae) although the latest DNA-based taxonomic research indicates that perhaps they should be treated separately. The 12 members of the family are restricted to the Oriental region and all except one is found in South-east Asia, but not east of Borneo. Ioras and leafbirds are all yellowish or greenish tree-dwelling birds that hop about in the tree canopy gleaning insects from the foliage; leafbirds also eat small fruits.*

Above: The COMMON IORA (Aegithina tiphia) as its name suggests is the most common of the ioras in its genus. It is widespread throughout the Oriental region, including the Philippines, and possibly owes its success to its adaptability. It occurs in all kinds of woodlands except primary forests: mangroves, secondary growth and even mature gardens in towns and cities are its home. It is a small, active bird that moves around in the small branches of trees picking off invertebrate prey, often while whistling softly. Here a female is seen at the tiny cup-shaped nest.

Right: The most widespread and numerous of the leafbirds, the BLUE-WINGED LEAFBIRD (Chloropsis cochinchinensis) can be found all over the Oriental region except the Philippines which has two endemic species of its own. Locally, it can be common in both primary and secondary forest, usually moving at canopy level but also sometimes descending almost to ground level at forest edges in search of insects, nectar or fruits. It is often seen in the company of other birds in fruiting fig trees or in passing flocks of insect-eaters — so-called bird waves.

Above: The GREATER GREEN LEAFBIRD (Chloropsis sonnerati) is endemic to Sunda, and is found mostly in primary and sometimes mature secondary rainforest where it stays in the canopy of large trees. It is a regular visitor to fruiting fig trees. This one is a female.

Below: The ORANGE-BELLIED LEAFBIRD (Chloropsis hardwickii) is a montane and submontane species found only between 600 and 2,000 metres. It is found from the Himalayas down into Thailand and Peninsular Malaysia where it can be quite common at hill stations. This is a male.

BULBULS

THE BULBULS (PYCNONOTIDAE) are perhaps the most conspicuous of all forest birds in South-east Asia. They form a large family that is well represented in the Oriental region: there are 36 species in Thailand, 27 in Malaysia, 10 in Singapore, 10 in the Philippines but only one in Indonesia east of Borneo. Unlike members of some other large families, for example babblers and thrushes, all of the family (except one northern Thai species) are known as bulbuls, with some descriptive composite adjective added in front. This makes understanding the family for beginners considerably easier. Bulbuls are also quite uniform in shape and colour – usually shades of brown, grey and yellow – and in fact some species are difficult to tell apart in the field. Their calls are not much help either, being varied clucking and chipping sounds that are difficult to recognize. Bulbuls are, however, fairly easy to view. Many species do well in selectively logged forest where they come out in the open at forest edges and trails feeding on fruits and insects from the canopy almost down to eye level. Seeing a large number of different bulbul species and reflecting on how they all differ in terms of habitat and behaviour is a satisfying part of birdwatching in South-east Asia.

Above: The YELLOW-VENTED BULBUL (*Pycnonotus goiavier*) occurs only in South-east Asia, in southern Thailand and the Philippines, but within this small range it is the most common of the bulbuls in coastal woodlands and mangroves and the only species in city parks and gardens. Its bubbling call can be heard from dawn in all villages of the region. Like most successful birds, it is omnivorous, sometimes feeding on fruits in the canopy of large trees, at other times grabbing insects in the grass.

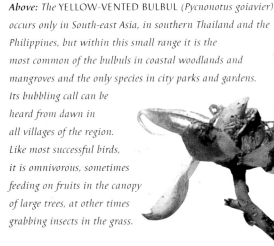

Right: The OLIVE-WINGED BULBUL (*Pycnonotus plumosus*) is restricted to the Sunda subregion extending into Palawan in the Philippines. It is locally common in lowland forest, especially secondary growth and coastal scrub.

Below: The YELLOW-BELLIED BULBUL *(Griniger phaeocephalus) is another species endemic to Sunda that is found only in the lowland rainforests of Peninsular Thailand, Malaysia, Borneo and Sumatra. It does well in primary and mature secondary forest and is an easy bird to see as it moves conspicuously through the mid-storey.*

Left: An adaptable species, the RED-WHISKERED BULBUL *(Pycnonotus jocosus) is native to the Oriental region, including Thailand and northern Peninsular Malaysia where it is a common bird in forest edges and villages, actively fluttering about, calling repeatedly and perching out in the open. It is a popular cage bird and has been introduced to countries like Singapore and Australia which are outside its range.*

Above: Endemic to Sunda and a lowland forest bird, the HAIRY-BACKED BULBUL *(Hypsipetes criniger) is locally common in overgrown forest edges near primary forest. It is sometimes seen closer to the ground than other bulbuls.*

Right: Most bulbuls are lowland birds, but the MOUNTAIN BULBUL *(Hypsipetes mcclellandii) is an Oriental region species that is found only in mountains, from 800 metres up to the tree-limit. It is distributed from the Himalayas into Thailand and Peninsular Malaysia where it is a very common bird at hill stations.*

Above: The STREAKED BULBUL *(Hypsipetes malaccensis) is endemic to Sunda. It is a large member of the family and appears less common than some of the other species. It stays high in the forest and rarely comes down to mid-storey, preferring the canopy of large trees where it often calls loudly and displays in small noisy groups.*

Right: The RED-EYED BULBUL *(Pycnonotus brunneus) is also endemic to Sunda and is typical of the humid, tropical forests in the Malaysian subregion. It occurs in primary forest as well as in secondary growth and forest edges, and is often seen visiting fruiting trees in the company of other species.*

Left: Widely distributed, the BLACK-CRESTED BULBUL (Pycnonotus melanicterus) is a montane species that occurs within a wide altitude range from the foothills across submontane forests to high summits. It can be found throughout most of the Oriental region including all of Thailand and the Sunda subregion, and is locally common in the right habitat.

Right: Apart from two escaped species on Sulawesi, the GOLDEN BULBUL (Ixos affinis) is the only bulbul to occur east of the Wallace's Line. The family does not extend into the Australasian region. Endemic to the Maluku province, it is an attractive bird, locally fairly common in forest and forest edges but like so many other Indonesian birds poorly studied and understood.

Above: The SPECTACLED BULBUL (Pycnonotus erythrophthalmos) has a red eye like the Red-eyed Bulbul, but can be distinguished from this species by its orange eye-ring and generally paler plumage. It is endemic to Sunda and is found in primary and secondary forest.

DRONGOS

DRONGOS (DICRURIDAE) ARE *medium-sized black or almost black birds with long forked tails. They constitute a small family that is well represented in South-east Asia. Drongos are tree-dwelling birds living in forests or open woodlands where they fly out from a perch to grab insects in mid-air. Consequently they are conspicuous birds, made more so by their loud, metallic calls that carry far. Some species are sedentary residents, others migrate.*

Below: *Strictly montane, the LESSER RACKET-TAILED DRONGO (Dicrurus remifer) takes over from the Greater Racket-tailed Drongo at hill stations and forest areas above 800 metres throughout the Oriental region, including Thailand, Peninsular Malaysia and Sumatra but excluding Borneo. Often seen in the company of other species, it is a primary forest bird that does not come out to the forest edges as much as other drongos. Note the different tail shape, a diagnostic feature when compared with the Greater Racket-tailed Drongo.*

Left: *The GREATER RACKET-TAILED DRONGO (Dicrurus paradiseus) occurs throughout the Oriental region including Thailand and the Sunda subregion where it is a common resident in primary forest, mangroves and disturbed woodlands. Usually seen in pairs, it is a bold species that will chase away other birds and even chase humans who enter its territory. It is very vocal, with a variety of whistles and screams, and often mixes in imitations of other birds' calls.*

Below: The ASHY DRONGO (*Dicrurus leucophaeus*) *varies in plumage from ashy grey to almost entirely black. It is widely distributed across the Oriental region, including the Philippines, in a wide variety of habitats from montane forests to lowland open country. It sits on an open perch from which it hawks for flying insects.*

Above: The BRONZED DRONGO (*Dicrurus aeneaus*) *is a small drongo with a characteristic glossy, metallic sheen to the plumage. Found throughout the Oriental region, including Thailand and the Sunda subregion, it is a forest bird living in primary and mature secondary lowland forest where it perches on exposed branches in the canopy or in open glades. Pairs are often seen together calling out and actively chasing one another.*

Below: The BLACK DRONGO (*Dicrocus macrocercus*) *is an Oriental region bird that is resident in Thailand and on Java/Bali, and a migrant to Malaysia and Singapore. It is a locally common bird in open country, marshes and cultivated areas, sitting on an open branch, pole or wire and flying out elegantly to grab insects in the air.*

CROWS

CROWS (CORVIDAE) MAY *not appear to be the most exciting of birds, but when investigated more closely they are seen to be a large family with some very successful species that have populated the world from the Arctic to the tropics. Crows are generally intelligent and omnivorous. Therefore several species have adapted to living close to people. Typical crows are large black birds with harsh calls, but there are also more colourful and delicate species in this family which includes the jay, magpie and treepie genera.*

Right: The BORNEO TREEPIE *(Dendrocitta cinerascens) is endemic to Borneo but is so similar to another treepie endemic to Sumatra (D. occipitalis) that some specialists treat them as the same species. Locally it can be fairly common in woodlands at submontane altitudes, for example at the Mount Kinabalu Park Headquarters in Sabah where it is often seen hopping through the trees on the lookout for invertebrate prey. Its calls are a varied series of metallic noises.*

Left: Magpies are attractive birds and the GREEN MAGPIE *(Cissa chinensis) is no exception. It may look conspicuous enough, but it is actually very difficult to spot as it hops through its montane rainforest home. Note how this one tries to hide behind the small twig. It is distributed throughout the mountainous parts of the Oriental region, from the Himalayas to Borneo. Here one has caught a small lizard.*

Right: The EURASIAN JAY (*Garrulus glandarius*), as the name indicates, is one of the birds that is shared between the Oriental and the western Palaearctic region which includes Europe. It reaches South-east Asia only in northern and western Thailand, where it can be a common bird locally in deciduous woodlands and open pine forests. It sits in low trees and often drops down to the ground to feed.

Below: Not all species of crows are widespread and numerous. This LONG-BILLED CROW (*Corvus validus*) is endemic to a small area in northern Maluku, Indonesia, where it is locally common in forest edges and near villages.

Above: Birds of paradise are fairly closely related to crows. They are an Australasian family of birds, but two species extend towards the Oriental region into the transitional zone of Wallacea where they are endemic to islands in the northern Maluku. The most spectacular of these is the STANDARD-WING BIRD OF PARADISE (*Semioptera wallacii*) which can be seen well on the island of Halmahera, but only at dawn when males congregate at certain trees in primary forest to display. Still poorly studied and little known, this species is regarded by scientists as near-threatened with extinction.

ORIOLES, NUTHATCHES AND TITS

ORIOLES (ORIOLIDAE) ARE *a small family of medium-sized, often colourful birds found in Asia and adjacent regions. They feed in the trees on fruits, nectar and insects. Orioles have soft, melodious calls that make them easy to locate, and they are often seen flying from tree to tree with a gently undulating flight-pattern. Nuthatches (Sittidae) are a small family of delightful little forest birds that run up and down tree trunks and thick branches gleaning insects from the bark. Tits (Paridae) are a large family of small birds poorly represented in South-east Asia where other bird families take their place. The Philippines has only three species, all of which are endemic; Malaysia has just two.*

Below: The BLACK-NAPED ORIOLE *(Oriolus chinensis) is an Oriental region bird that is found as a resident or migrant all over South-east Asia, including the Philippines and extending into Sulawesi and Nusa Tenggara in eastern Indonesia. Singapore is a good place to see it; even in the city you can hear its loud fluty call above the traffic noise. Locally it is common in coastal forests, forest edges, orchards, villages and parks. The nest is a small cup built in a forked branch high in a tree. This is a male.*

Above: The fairy-bluebirds are sometimes treated as part of the oriole family, sometimes as leafbirds and sometimes in their own family (Irenidae). There are only two members in this family, both in the Oriental region: a species endemic to the Philippines and this one, the ASIAN FAIRY-BLUEBIRD *(Irena puella), which is widespread throughout the region including all of South-east Asia. It is a primary lowland-forest bird, which sometimes extends into mature secondary forest if there are enough huge trees, as it likes to move at canopy level. It is often seen in fruiting fig trees or flying across the forest while whistling loudly. This is a male; the female is uniformly dull blue.*

DUSKY ORIOLE
(Oriolus phaeochromus)

There are several orioles endemic to eastern Indonesia and the Dusky Oriole is one of them. It is only found on the island of Halmahera in Maluku. Virtually nothing is known about this bird and it has never been photographed before. This one has just grabbed a spider.

Right: The VELVET-FRONTED NUTHATCH (Sitta frontalis) is widely distributed in the Oriental region and occurs all over South-east Asia, including the Philippines. It can be found in primary lowland forest, and is locally a fairly common bird, always on the move in a constant, frantic search for food as this photograph of a male shows.

Above: The GREAT TIT (Parus major) has a patchy distribution in South-east Asia and is the only member of the family to extend east into parts of Nusa Tenggara in Indonesia. While this is a common garden bird at feeding tables in Europe, in Thailand it is a montane forest bird and in the Sunda subregion it is found in coastal mangroves.

BABBLERS

THE BABBLERS (TIMALIIDAE) *constitute one of the most successful and diverse bird families in the Oriental region. Most babblers are typical rainforest birds, resident all year and fairly sedentary. In Peninsular Malaysia alone there are 46 different species. On the island of Borneo there are 36 babblers, while on Sulawesi, just east of there but on the other side of Wallace's Line, there is only one!*

To casual birdwatchers in the forest, the babblers present a difficult problem as the various species are typically skulkers that move quickly through the dark undergrowth. Many species are similar-looking, medium-sized brown and grey birds. Their calls are often diagnostic but they take a long time to memorize accurately. Identification is hence a real challenge. However, to serious ornithologists the babblers are one of the most fascinating families to watch. Many species are rare in the forest, so it takes years to see most of the members of this family; very few people have seen them all.

Below: Perhaps the prettiest of all babblers, the SILVER-EARED MESIA (Leiothrix argentauris) is locally common in forested hills of the region including Thailand, Peninsular Malaysia and Sumatra. An active bird, it moves low through forest edges in little groups, never staying long in one place.

Left: The WHITE-CHESTED BABBLER (Trichastoma rostratum) is a small, skulking rainforest bird, often found near a stream or a flooded part of the forest. It moves low, near or on the ground. It usually calls very early in the morning at daybreak and will respond to a taped playback of its call. Used sparingly, this can be a good method of seeing this elusive babbler, and others like it, well.

Babblers vary tremendously in appearance, from the diminutive ground dwellers like the Pigmy Wren-babbler to the colourful Silver-eared Mesia and the much larger Long-tailed Sibia. Babblers have a mainly insectivorous diet, and the family is well represented in the highlands of the region, many species only being found in montane rainforest above 1,000 metres.

Below: The SCALY-CROWNED BABBLER *(Malacopteron cinereum) is restricted in distribution to parts of Thailand and the Sunda subregion. Locally it is a fairly regular babbler in lowland primary and mature secondary forest, always on the move, hopping low among the trees, calling softly.*

Above: The PIGMY WREN-BABBLER *(Pnoepyga pusilla) is one of them; it is widely distributed from the Himalayas to South-east Asia except Borneo. Apart from an endemic species on Sulawesi, it is also the only member of the family east of Wallace's Line, its distribution extending from Java into Flores and Timor in eastern Indonesia. At just 9 centimetres long it is one of the smallest birds in South-east Asia. Scuttling across the dark forest floor, this one is carrying nesting material.*

Right: It is hard to believe but this LONG-TAILED SIBIA *(Heterophasia picaoides) belongs to the same family as the Pigmy Wren-Babbler (above)! It is quite common through parts of the Oriental region, including Thailand, Peninsular Malaysia and Sumatra. It is found only between 900 and 1,800 metres where it moves at mid-storey in forests and gardens, always on the move in small groups, individuals chattering softly to each other.*

Above: Widely distributed throughout forested montains in the Himalayas and South-east Asia, the GREY-THROATED BABBLER (Stachyris nigriceps) belongs to one of the so-called tree-babbler genera; typical of these it skulks low in the forest undergrowth, a metre off the ground, never sitting still in one place and therefore difficult to see well.

Laughingthrushes are large, vocal babblers that feed on or near the ground. Many have Himalayan affinities but not the CHESTNUT-CAPPED LAUGHINGTHRUSH (Garrulax mitratus), which occurs only in Peninsular Malaysia, Borneo and Sumatra. Locally, it can be a very common bird in submontane forests between 700 and 2,000 metres. The Peninsular race (**above**) differs in its head pattern from the Borneo race (**right**).

Above: Like the Silver-eared Mesia, yuhinas are a genus among the so-called song-babblers. The CHESTNUT-CRESTED YUHINA (*Yuhina everetti*) is endemic to Borneo where it can often be seen around the Kinabalu Park Headquarters moving through the low storey of the forest in chattering groups.

Above: The SOOTY-CAPPED BABBLER (*Malacopteron affine*) is endemic to lowland forests in the Sunda subregion. Like other members of the Malacopteron genus, it moves slightly higher in the closed forest than some babblers, from low storey to lower mid-storey a few metres off the ground. It has a hesitant, penetrating, almost 'human' whistle.

Top: Strictly montane, the BLUE-WINGED MINLA (*Minla cyanouroptera*) is locally a common babbler in the Oriental region including elevated parts of Thailand and Peninsular Malaysia. It moves with other insect-eaters through the forest in active and vocal groups.

Above: Found only in Thailand, Peninsular Malaysia and parts of Indochina, the MOUNTAIN FULVETTA (*Alcippe peracensis*) is a typical babbler, skulking low in the submontane forest, often seen with other species in constantly moving, mixed flocks.

Left: Rich in rainforest birds, Malaysia is home to no less than 55 members of the babbler family, among them this CHESTNUT-RUMPED BABBLER (Stachyris maculata), which is found only in the Sunda subregion. It is a secretive ground- and mid-storey species, but it can be brought into view early in the morning if you mimic its call.

Right: Amazingly, of the 19 species of babblers found in the Philippines, all except one are endemic to that country. The exception is this species, the STRIPED TIT-BABBLER (Macronous gularis), which is widespread throughout the Oriental region including all of South-east Asia. Although a forest bird, is seems to prefer secondary growth and overgrown clearings where it hops about low in the scrub, always a few together chattering constantly with slurred, soft calls.

Left: Babblers feed by gleaning insects from the foliage as this CHESTNUT-WINGED BABBLER (Stachyris erythroptera) is doing. It is a forest bird endemic to Sunda.

THRUSHES

THE THRUSHES (TURDIDAE) are a large, very diverse family of birds. Apart from true thrushes, the family includes shortwings, robins, forktails, chats and several other bird types. The thrushes do particularly well in subtropical and temperate climate zones. Therefore Thailand has many resident species, whereas the equatorial Sunda subregion has fewer. However, many of the northern species migrate and can be found as winter visitors in South-east Asia.

Above: In contrast to chats, shortwings are skulking birds of the forest floor, almost wren-babbler-like in demeanor. The WHITE-BROWED SHORTWING (Brachypteryx montana) can be found only in upper montane habitats from 1,400 metres up to the tree-line, often near little forest streams. Although widely distributed throughout mountains in South-east Asia, including the Philippines, it is a secretive bird that is not easy to view well. This is an immature bird.

Pete Morris

Below : The PIED BUSHCHAT (Saxicola caprata) has a wide distribution from west Asia to the island of New Guinea, but since it is an open country, grassland bird it avoids the Sunda subregion. In South-east Asia it is therefore only found in central and northern Thailand, the Philippines and then from Java and Bali eastwards through Indonesia. Locally it can be common in open woodlands and cultivated areas, always sitting on an exposed perch flying into the air or to the ground to grab insects. This is a male; the female is dull brown.

Left: The BLACK-BREASTED FRUIT-HUNTER (Chlamydochaera jefferyi) is sometimes included in the oriole family and sometimes with the cuckoo-shrikes. Lately it has been identified as a thrush and yet it behaves like a pigeon! Rarely seen, it is endemic to Borneo and is known only from Mount Kinabalu and a few other mountains in the north. The bird's nest has never been found. This rare photograph shows a male.

Left: THE MAGPIE ROBIN (*Copsychus saularis*) is a widespread Oriental region bird. Common throughout South-east Asia, it is less common in the Philippines and does not cross Wallace's Line. It is mainly a park and village bird extending into open woodlands, forest edges and logging camps, but it is never found in mature forest. Like many thrushes, it is a delightful songster, and for that reason it is a popular cage bird. Capture for this trade has caused a decline in the natural populations. This is a male; in the female the black parts of the plumage are replaced by slaty grey.

Above: Among the true thrushes, the MOUNTAIN BLACKBIRD (*Turdus poliocephalus*) has a peculiar status as it is the only member of the otherwise temperate *Turdus* genus to breed in tropical Malaysia and Indonesia. There it is an upper montane bird, locally common in forested hills on Borneo, Java and Sumatra, living from 2,000 metres all the way up to the tree line at 3,400 metres. It also occurs in the Philippines, north to Taiwan and east to islands in the Pacific where it is a coastal bird!

WARBLERS

'WARBLERS' IS A *broad term for members of the Sylviidae family which includes leaf-warblers, bush-warblers, reed-warblers, grass-warblers, prinias, tailorbirds, tesias and a few other varieties. All warblers, however, are small birds with thin, sharp beaks, good for catching the insects and larvae that they all feed upon. Some species are tree-dwelling forest birds, but many others live in open country or marshes. Northern warblers migrate south in winter but the Oriental region species are sedentary.*

Below: The ZITTING CISTICOLA (Cisticola juncidis) is a grass-warbler. It has a typically streaked plumage and is found in open countryside, paddy-fields and often near marshes, plains or wherever tall grass grows. It has a wide distribution and is locally common throughout South-east Asia, including the Philippines and eastern Indonesia, but is absent from Borneo.

Right: The tailorbirds in the Orthotomus genus are some of the most successful of all Oriental birds found throughout the region including all of South-east Asia. The COMMON TAILORBIRD (Orthotomus sutorius) is the dominant species in light forest, scrub and gardens in Thailand, Peninsular Malaysia and Singapore. In Indonesia, other tailorbirds take over, as in the Philippines, where there are eight other tailorbirds in all, five of which are endemic to that country. Like all tailorbirds, the Common builds its nest inside a pouch made from one or two leaves, 'stitched' together with straw and spiders web.

Ong Kiem Sian

Above: The SUNDA BUSH-WARBLER (*Cettia vulcania*) is a montane warbler that hops about babbler-style low in the dense moss-covered forests of the upper montane region above 1,500 metres. Locally common on Sumatra, Borneo and Java, it is quite a regular bird in the high mountains and it may in fact form one species with a similar, more widespread Oriental region species, *C. fortipes*.

Right: Prinias are mainly open-country warblers. The YELLOW-BELLIED PRINIA (*Prinia flaviventris*) is found in tall grass areas both near marshes and in open scrub in drier terrain. It is common in that habitat throughout most parts of South-east Asia. Like other warblers, it is very vocal with a characteristic bubbling call that it performs from the top of a grass stem or low bush.

Left: As the name suggests, the ORIENTAL REED-WARBLER (*Acrocephalus orientalis*) is found mainly in reed beds, marshes and sometimes adjacent scrub. Breeding in east Asia, this species is only a winter visitor to South-east Asia, but it turns up in all the countries and during peak migration periods it is locally very numerous, its loud warning call being heard from all directions.

*F*LYCATCHERS

THE FLYCATCHERS (MUSCICAPIDAE) *are a large family of small birds that sit upright on a perch flying out to grab insects in the air, which makes them fairly easy to spot and observe. The family is well represented in the Oriental region and in South-east Asia. Only a few species extend into eastern Indonesia where some similar Australasian families take over the flycatcher role. All flycatchers are tree-dwelling – many are denizens of primary forest, others prefer open woodlands. Some northern species migrate and appear in the tropics as winter visitors only.*

Above: Whistlers (Pachycephalidae) are a large family of mainly Australasian species. They are more robust in build than the flycatchers to which they are somewhat related. Only a few penetrate into South-east Asia. The BORNEAN WHISTLER *(Pachycephala hypoxantha) is endemic to Borneo and is locally common in montane forest habitat between 900 and 2,600 metres, such as at the Kinabalu Park Headquarters.*

Right: The INDIGO FLYCATCHER *(Eumyias indigo) is found only on Borneo, Sumatra and Java where it is a montane bird in forest at 900—3,000 metres. This pretty bird can be seen well at the Kinabalu Park Headquarters, where it comes out onto the trails early in the morning together with other birds to feed on moths at the outdoor lamps.*

Below: *Like babblers, flycatchers do well in submontane forest with many insects. This* LITTLE PIED FLYCATCHER *(Ficedula westermanni) is a particularly successful species occurring throughout the Oriental region including South-east Asia and the Philippines and Wallacea, wherever there are forested hills between 700 and 2,600 metres. This is a male; the female has uniform brown upperparts.*

Above: *This male* GOLDEN WHISTLER *(Pachycephala pectoralis) is an Australian forest bird that occurs as far west as Bali and Java. It is locally common throughout eastern Indonesia.*

Above: *The* FERRUGINOUS FLYCATCHER *(Muscicapa ferruginea) is one of the migratory flycatchers that comes down from east Asia during the northern winter. It is a tiny bird occurring in small numbers throughout South-east Asia in lowland and submontane forest where it hawks for insects from a low perch.*

Below: The SNOWY-BROWED FLYCATCHER (*Ficedula hyperythra*) has a similar distribution to the Little Pied Flycatcher, but it is even more of a montane species as its range extends up to the tree limit above 3,000 metres at the highest peaks of the region. It sits low in the montane forest, where this attractive bird is easily overlooked, and from its perch it jumps down onto the ground to feed.

Above: The male LARGE NILTAVA (*Niltava grandis*) shown here is a large, handsome flycatcher; the female is uniformly brown. It occurs in montane forest above 900 metres from the Himalayas into Thailand, Peninsular Malaysia and Sumatra in South-east Asia.

Right: The Rhinomyias flycatchers are, true to their name, 'jungle-flycatchers'. Always found inside primary and mature secondary forest, their lifestyle is such that they never become really numerous. The GREY-CHESTED FLYCATCHER (*Rhinomyias umbratilis*) lives in lowland forests in the Sunda subregion, but it is nowhere common. Shy and staying low near the undergrowth it is not easy to observe. It was captured in a photograph for the first time only in 1995 when this photograph was published in the British magazine Birdwatch.

Above left: The MANGROVE BLUE FLYCATCHER *(Cyornis rufigastra) is a true mangrove bird in most of its range, especially in the Sunda subregion. There it resides at the tidal edge of the mangroves, and in Nipa palm areas, hunting for insects close to or on the mudflats. It also occurs in the Philippines and on some Indonesian islands, there also living behind the coast in secondary growth and forest edges.*

Above right: Monarch flycatchers are placed in their own family (Monarchidae) by most specialists. They are medium-sized birds sallying for insects in the air or gleaning them from the foliage. The RUFOUS-WINGED FLYCATCHER *(Philentoma pyrhopterum) is a member of this family endemic to the Sunda subregion. It is a forest bird moving in the middle storey of primary and mature secondary forest and is locally quite a regular bird in the right habitat. This is a male.*

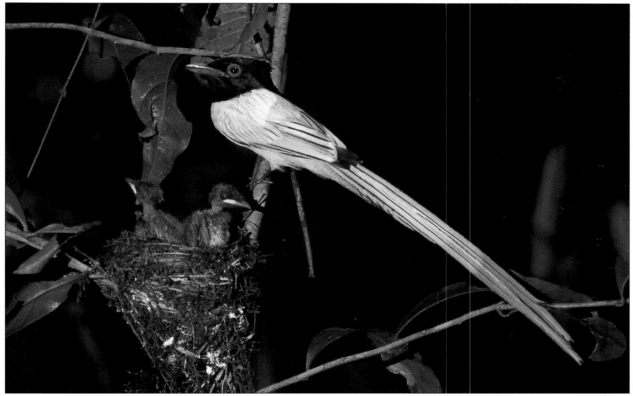

Above: The ASIAN PARADISE-FLYCATCHER *(Terpsiphone atrocaudata) is another member of the Monarch family. It is a widespread resident and migrant in the Oriental region, including Thailand and the Sunda subregion. Mature males develop long tail feathers and sometimes a spectacular white mantle as this individual shows at its nest.*

87

PIPITS AND OTHERS

PIPITS (MOTACILLIDAE), SHRIKES *(Laniidae)*, white-eyes *(Zosteropidae)* and wood-swallows *(Artamidae)* bear little resemblance to one another and have been grouped here for convenience. There is only one resident member of the pipit family in the region, Richard's Pipit *(Anthus novaeseelandiae)*. Several wagtails, which are also part of this family, occur here, but they are all migrant visitors. The shrikes are medium-sized birds that frequent open country and wooded areas. Only a handful of species are found in South-east Asia, but they are conspicuous birds sitting quietly out in the open even in the mid-day sun, looking for insects and small lizards in the long grass below.

Pete Morris

Top: Not all white-eyes have white eyes – some have black, like this MOUNTAIN BLACK-EYE (Chlorocharis emiliae) which is endemic to northern Borneo. It is an upper montane bird that is quite common at Mount Kinabalu, where it is usually the last bird to be seen before the end of the vegetation at about 3,500 metres.

Above: RICHARD'S PIPIT (Anthus novaeseelandiae) has a very wide distribution from Africa across most of Asia and into Australia. It is a common resident and a migrant to South-east Asia, and during peak migration it can be numerous locally. The resident race is sometimes treated as a separate species, the PADDYFIELD PIPIT (A. rufulus). It is a typical open-country bird, found in short-grass coastal terrain, cultivated fields and also montane meadows. It seldom perches in trees, preferring to run on the ground in search of prey. When disturbed, it flies off in an undulating flight pattern giving a harsh chipping call.

White-eyes are a large family of greenish, warbler-like birds. They are active creatures, often seen in flocks, constantly searching the trees for insects and small fruits. The family is well represented in both the Oriental and especially the Australasian regions: Indonesia has 31 species, Thailand only four. Some white-eyes are very similar and difficult to identify in the field.

WHITE-BREASTED WOOD-SWALLOW (*Artamus leucorhynchus*)

Wood-swallows are a small, mainly Australasian, family of birds. There are just two species in South-east Asia. The White-breasted Wood-Swallow is the only widespread member of the family, occurring from Australia, throughout Indonesia and into the Philippines and Peninsular Malaysia. Locally it is a common bird near the coast or in open woodlands further inland. It sits on an exposed branch, from which it makes short flights like a bee-eater, flapping and gliding intermittently and catching insects while in the air. A few birds are always seen together, often displaying and calling softly to one another.

Left: The GREY WAGTAIL (Motacilla cinerea) is a common migrant throughout the whole region, which is always found near water, often in forested areas near mountain streams, but also at montane altitudes. It runs restlessly around near the water s edge or on trails nearby, constantly wagging its tail as its name implies.

Right: More of a forest bird than other shrikes, the TIGER SHRIKE (Lanius tigrinus), named after its barred plumage, is a migrant to South-east Asia from its breeding grounds as far north as China and Japan. It can be seen in Thailand, the Philippines and part of the Sunda subregion, but it is less common than the Brown Shrike and less conspicuous, mostly staying in dense cover in forest and forest edges; its chattering call might give it away.

S TARLINGS

STARLINGS AND MYNAS *all belong to the family Sturnidae, which holds some of the more successful and widespread species in South-east Asia – and also some of the more localized and endangered ones. Starlings are gregarious birds that often nest in colonies; outside the breeding season they gather at large communal roosts. They are vocal and conspicuous birds, feeding either on fruits in the trees or on invertebrates on the ground where they walk along briskly – not hopping like many other birds.*

Left: The HILL MYNA (Gracula religiosa) is widespread throughout the Oriental region including all of South-east Asia except eastern Indonesia. It is a large starling found in primary and mature secondary forest, coastal woodlands and coconut plantations. It often sits on a high perch in a huge tree whistling loudly and mimicking other sounds, or pairs may be seen together flying high over the forest. Although still locally common, it has declined in numbers recently due to forest clearance and trapping for the wild-bird trade. It is easy to keep and popular with collectors as it can learn to 'talk'.

Right: Mynas are among the most numerous birds in South-east Asia. This species, the COMMON MYNA (Acridotheres tristis), is a widespread Oriental region bird that is extremely numerous in Thailand, Peninsular Malaysia and Singapore. Although absent from the Philippines, there are local populations in Indonesia, probably from escaped cage birds. It prefers cultivation and urban environments, often walking on the ground near foodstalls or even entering houses to grab food. Totally omnivorous, intelligent and bold, it has all the traits necessary to succeed in an 'un-natural' world.

Right: The PHILIPPINE GLOSSY STARLING *(Aplonis panayensis) is widespread throughout South-east Asia, including the Philippines and parts of eastern Indonesia. It is an adaptable open-woodlands bird that has benefited from the extensive forest clearance in the region. Now it is very common in gardens, parks, and on roadsides. Its nest is often built under roofs in buildings, but also in tree cavities or inside dense epiphytes. It does not come down on the ground as much as some mynas, preferring instead to stay in the trees where it feeds mainly on fruits of all kinds. The one in this picture is feeding on a papaya.*

Below: While the Philippine Glossy Starling builds its nest in cavities, like most other starlings the closely related ISLAND STARLING *(Aplonis mysolensis) builds its nest in the open in dense communal clumps in large trees. This species is found only on islands in eastern Indonesia.*

SUNBIRDS

THE SUNBIRDS (NECTARINIIDAE) *are a large family of attractive and often numerous birds sometimes confused by many garden-owners in the region with hummingbirds. However, hummingbirds occur only in the Americas while sunbirds occupy much the same niche in Africa and the Oriental region. Only two species extend into the Australasian region where honeyeaters (Meliphagidae) are otherwise the predominant family of*

nectar-feeders. Sunbirds are small and active birds, always on the move flitting from flower to flower and quickly extracting the nectar with their long beaks and tongues. Males especially have scintillating, metallic colours that shine in the sun. True to their name, sunbirds are late risers, mainly active in the bright morning sun from 9am until noon.

Above left: A male PURPLE-THROATED SUNBIRD *(Nectarinia sperata) clearly displays the reason for its name. This sunbird is widespread in mangroves and forest edges, and sometimes also in parks and gardens throughout South-east Asia including the Philippines and parts of eastern Indonesia. It is not, however, very common.*

Left: As this picture of a female CRIMSON SUNBIRD *(Aethopyga siparaja) shows, sunbirds sometimes 'steal' the nectar by penetrating a flower from the side, thereby destroying it without participating in the pollination process.*

Left: Sunbirds seem to have a preference for red flowers; this is a male BROWN-THROATED SUNBIRD (*Anthreptes malacensis*). This species is a bit larger and slower than the Olive-backed Sunbird and is not as widespread, but locally it is almost as common throughout all of South-east Asia. It can be found in rural gardens and parks, and also coconut plantations and secondary forest edges.

Above: The most widespread of all the sunbirds, the OLIVE-BACKED SUNBIRD (*Nectarinia jugularis*) is common in all South-east Asian countries including Indonesia. It is in fact one of the most characteristic birds of the whole region. It feeds well on ornamental flowers and is therefore often seen in parks and gardens, and even on potted plants on high-rise apartment balconies, where it has also been known to build its pouch-type nest suspended from a twig.

Above: Maybe the prettiest of them all: the male CRIMSON SUNBIRD (*Aethopyga siparaja*) is found in all the South-east Asian countries in forest edges and plantations. Sometimes it turns up in gardens but not as predictably as some of the other species.

Above: Honeyeaters (Meliphagidae) are a large and diverse family of Australasian region birds. There are no less than 77 species found in Indonesia, most of which occur on Irian Jaya, but many others are endemic to isolated islands. Only one species extends west out of Wallacea and into the Oriental region, and that is the widespread BROWN HONEYEATER (Lichmera indistincta). The Indonesian variety is treated by MacKinnon & Phillipps (1993) as an endemic species, the INDONESIAN HONEYEATER (L. limbata). For some reason just this bird has crossed Wallace's Line to Bali where it is locally common in forest edges, sometimes also feeding on ornamental plants in parks and gardens.

Left: The BLACK SUNBIRD (Nectarinia aspasia) is distributed on islands in eastern Indonesia into New Guinea but is not found west of Wallace's Line. Locally it is a common bird in forest edges, plantations and gardens where it adds a lively and appealing element to the environment.

Right: Occasionally sunbirds will take tiny insects on their rounds and also small fruits as this picture of a RED-THROATED SUNBIRD (Anthreptes rhodolaema) shows. Superficially similar to the Brown-throated Sunbird, this species takes over as a forest bird endemic to the Sunda subregion and is found only in small numbers inside primary and mature secondary lowland forest.

Above: While visiting flowers, sunbirds participate in the pollination process. Note the pollen being deposited on this immature BROWN-THROATED SUNBIRD'S (Anthreptes malacensis) forehead.

Right: Spiderhunters form a special genus of the sunbird family. They are larger, have exceptionally long bills and take many spiders and other invertebrates as well as nectar; the sexes are similar. Restricted to the Oriental region, several species occur here. All are forest birds that often move high in the trees at canopy level. The STREAKED SPIDERHUNTER (Arachnothera magna) is a montane bird found at 600–1,800 metres in the Himalayas and into Thailand and Peninsular Malaysia hill stations where it is locally very common in forest, forest edges and gardens.

Left: In the montane habitat there are few sunbirds, but this species, the BLACK-THROATED SUNBIRD (Aethopyga saturata), here a male, can be found only at submontane elevations between 300 and 1,700 metres. An Oriental region bird, it occurs from the Himalayas and into Thailand and Peninsular Malaysia but is not found anywhere else in South-east Asia. Locally it is very common in forested hills, both inside primary forest and in forest edges and nearby gardens.

FLOWERPECKERS

FLOWERPECKERS (DICAEDAE) ARE *the smallest birds in the region, being only 8–10 centimetres long. Like sunbirds, they feed on flowering trees, but they do not extract nectar, rather they pick out fruits and tiny insects, their short, strong bills being well suited for this job. Many species are especially fond of parasitic mistletoe plants. Flowerpeckers often feed in the canopy of large trees, but at forest edges they will also come down to eye-level. They fly in a jerky, abrupt manner, constantly emitting a high-pitched ticking call that seems to be common to all species. The family is widely distributed throughout both the Oriental and the Australasian regions, although many species are localized; out of the 14 flowerpeckers occurring in the Philippines, for instance, all but two are endemic to that country.*

Above: The YELLOW-VENTED FLOWERPECKER (*Diacaeum chrysorrheum*) *occurs throughout South-east Asia east to Wallace's Line. It feeds on small fruits and insect larvae that it picks out from tall trees and low bushes in or near lowland forest.*

*Most flowerpeckers are sexually dimorphic, that is the two sexes have different plumages. Here is a male (**above**) and a female (**right**) CRIMSON-BREASTED FLOWERPECKER (Prionochilus percussus), an endemic to Sunda found only in lowland forest. Among flowerpeckers, the females and juveniles of different species can be difficult, or impossible, to tell apart in the field. Luckily pairs and families usually move about together.*

Below: The YELLOW-BREASTED FLOWERPECKER (*Prionochilus maculatus*) is a species endemic to Sunda. It is locally common throughout the subregion, but is extinct in Singapore. It favours primary and mature secondary forest and often comes out at overgrown logging trails to feed low on rhododendron fruits.

Below left: The ORANGE-BELLIED FLOWERPECKER (*Dicaeum trigonostigma*) is the most widespread of the flowerpeckers and is locally common throughout South-east Asia including the Philippines. It is found in lowland forest, especially in forest edges and secondary growth near primary forest. Usually feeding in the highest canopies, it sometimes comes down near the ground and unlike other forest birds it can be quite approachable. The male plumage is amazing when you see it close up for the first time.

Above: Only one flowerpecker in South-east Asia is not a forest bird and that is the SCARLET-BACKED FLOWERPECKER (*Dicaeum cruentatum*). This pretty bird (here a male) occurs throughout the Oriental region, including Thailand and the Sunda subregion where it is common in open woodlands, parks and gardens. It is, however, not easy to view well, as it is always on the move high in the trees. You might catch a glimpse of one when it moves to a new tree flying rapidly and calling with metallic clicks.

Right: The JAVA SPARROW (Padda oryzivora) is a large member of the munia family. Although endemic to Java and Bali, it is heavily persecuted there because of its taste for rice and because it is a valuable cage bird. Formerly abundant, it is now so scarce within its natural range that BirdLife International regards this species as vulnerable to extinction. However, it does well in captivity and escaped birds have established themselves successfully in other parts of Indonesia, as well as in Singapore, Thailand and the Philippines.

W EAVERS

WEAVERS (PLOCEIDAE) ARE *a large family of mainly seed-eating birds, which are very numerous in open-country grasslands and savanna habitat. This type of terrain is not dominant in South-east Asia, but some species occur in coastal regions, wetlands and forest edges and they have generally benefited from developments and intensive forest clearance. Feeding on grain and cereals, weavers are attracted to agricultural regions and paddy-fields where they are regarded as pests. The family consists of three groups, which are split into separate families by some specialists: munias, sparrows and weavers. All are easy to keep in captivity, and therefore many species are popular cage birds. Some escape and establish feral populations outside their original range.*

Above: Sometimes placed with weavers and sometimes in their own family (Passeridae), sparrows are not well represented in South-east Asia. In fact only one species, the EURASIAN TREE-SPARROW (Passer montanus), plays any significant role amongst the birds there. This European/Asian species is now a numerous bird throughout all the countries in the region having spread naturally or by introduction. It is the only bird in the region that depends entirely on humans for survival; it lives only in villages and towns where it feeds on grain and food scraps. The nest is built in cavities in buildings.

Right: Weavers are absent from the Philippines and eastern Indonesia, but three species occur in Thailand and the Sunda subregion. The BAYA WEAVER (Ploceus philippinus) is locally common throughout Thailand, Peninsular Malaysia, Singapore and Sumatra. It is always found in open countryside, which is usually marshy, with tall grass and scrub, scattered trees and coconut palms. Here it builds a finely woven nest suspended from the branches and leaves. The photograph shows a male putting the finishing touches to his work. A weaver nesting colony at peak activity is one of South-east Asia's great birdwatching spectacles.

STREAKED WEAVER
(Ploceus manyar)

The Streaked Weaver is the predominant weaver on Java and Bali, but is generally less common in Thailand. It builds its nest lower than the Baya Weaver, in tall grass and low bushes. The nest is not quite as elaborately constructed, but the male is still proud of his achievement and tries to lure a female close with active displays, bashing of wings and chattering calls. The picture sequence shows how the fresh straws are woven into place.

Left: Among the munias, sometimes treated in their own family (Estrildidae), the SCALY-BREASTED MUNIA (Lonchura punctulata) is the most widespread and numerous. It occurs throughout the whole of the Oriental region including South-east Asia, the Philippines and into parts of eastern Indonesia. Feral populations have now established themselves in Australia and Hawaii among other places. It is seen in all kinds of open country, grasslands and cultivation, often feeding in the tall grass near rural roadsides.

T HAILAND

THAILAND IS ONE *of the more popular places to visit among the international birdwatching and eco-tourist jet-set. The friendly and courteous people, the reliable infrastructure and good visitors' facilities (in spite of the notorious traffic jams of Bangkok), plus a good network of well-managed national parks guarantee a pleasant experience.*

And of course there are the birds. Nobody comes back disappointed from an early morning spent birdwatching at Khao Yai National Park, the oldest and still the most popular of the parks. Yet consider this: 95 per cent of observations at Khao Yai have been conducted in a 20 square kilometre area surrounding the park headquarters. The other 2,148 square kilometres of the park have hardly been surveyed at all!

In the north-west of the country, the Doi Inthanon and the Doi Suthep-Pui National parks, close to the city of Chiang Mai, hold a different bird life with many montane species, some with Himalayan affinities. Then in the other corner of the country, in the very south, Thale Ban

Above: *The* BLUE-BEARDED BEE-EATER *Nyctyornis athertoni is in the same genus as the Red-bearded (see page 46), but it only occurs in the northern parts of the Oriental region, so Thailand is the southern limit for this as well as a number of other subtropical species.*

Above: *Khao Yai National Park.*

Right: *In this region the* SPECTACLED BARWING *(Actinodura ramsayi) from the babbler family is found only in the pine and oak forests at Doi Chiang Dao in northern Thailand. This sub-tropical type of vegetation is not found further south in South-east Asia.*

National Park is populated by yet another set of birds, many shared with nearby Malaysia.

There are 63 national parks and 32 wildlife sanctuaries in Thailand, covering over 11 per cent of the country. It would therefore appear that the birds of Thailand are protected and doing well, but this is not the whole story. Forest cover has declined rapidly this century, especially during the last few decades, from 60 per cent in the 1950s to less than 20 per cent today. Much of what is left is fragmented and degraded. Although commercial logging operations were outlawed by the government in 1989, illegal logging, clearance by farmers and settlers, and deliberate fires continue to destroy the forest. In southern Thailand, very little lowland rainforest is left and most of the birds of the Sunda subregion that boost the Thai checklist are in fact now very difficult to find in the field.

The complex system of different climate zones, habitats and zoogeographical subregions gives Thailand a diverse bird life and a long checklist, although it has no endemics except for Deignan's Babbler (*Stachyris rodolphei*) and the possibly extinct White-eyed River-martin (*Pseudochelidon sirintarae*). Today, outside (and even often inside) the protected areas there is still a lot of pressure on the land, and many birds are declining rapidly in numbers.

A special feature of birdwatching in Thailand is the book that you have at your disposal, *A Guide to the Birds of Thailand*. It is the best field guide available in Asia and a wonderful tool for identifying all the species that you will encounter there.

The PURPLE SUNBIRD *(Nectarinia asiatica) is distributed throughout the Middle East and south Asia. It prefers deciduous woodlands and open scrubland for habitat. In central Thailand, it is a common garden and park bird, but it does not occur further south.*

BIRDS OF THAILAND AT A GLANCE

Number of species:	915
Number of endemics:	2
Number of threatened species:	44
Data deficient:	1
Near threatened:	57

Useful field-identification guides:
A Guide to the Birds of Thailand, Boonsong Lekagul and Philip D. Round. Saha Karn Bhaet, 1991.

A Photographic Guide to Birds of Thailand, M. Webster. New Holland, 1997.

Check-lists:
Birds of Doi Inthanon National Park, Mahidol University, 1989.

Birds of Khao Yai National Park, Mahidol University, 1989.

Useful site-guides:
National Parks of Thailand, Mark Graham. Communications Resources, 1991.

A Birders' Guide to Thailand, K. Taylor. Canada, 1993.

Useful address:
Bird Conservation Society of Thailand
PO Box 13
Rajathavee PO
Bangkok 10401
Thailand

Goran Ekstrom/Windrush Photos

M ALAYSIA

MALAYSIA AS A *national entity does not have many endemic birds, but it is regarded amongst birdwatchers as probably the best place to see the 129 species that are restricted to the Sunda subregion.*

Above: Birdwatching in the mangroves.

M ost of the species endemic to Sunda are rainforest species, and on Peninsular Malaysia there are easy access points to the lowland rainforest at Templer's Park near Kuala Lumpur, at the National Park of Taman Negara in the state of Pahang and at Endau-Rompin State Park in Johor. For montane birds only occurring in forests above 900 metres or so, the three main hill stations (at Cameron Highlands, Genting and Fraser's Hill) provide convenient vantage points for some of the best birdwatching South-east Asia has to offer.
In the two East Malaysian states of Sabah and Sarawak, the special birds occurring only on Borneo are largely shared with the two other nations with a stake on the island – the small kingdom of Brunei and the province of Kalimantan, a part of Indonesia. However, most birdwatchers find themselves travelling to the Malaysian part of the island to see the good birds, especially to Sabah, where the Kinabalu National Park is most popular for montane species. The nearby Poring Hot Springs and further inland the Danum Valley Field Centre are good places to find the lowland rainforest birds. The giant Mulu National Park in Sarawak is another important eco-tourism destination, but birds are harder to see well there. While the absolutely fascinating

BIRDS OF MALAYSIA AT A GLANCE

Number of species:	*Peninsular Malaysia*	638
	East Malaysia	570
	Whole country	725
Number of endemics:	*Peninsular Malaysia*	2
	Borneo	31
Number of threatened species:		31
Data deficient:		4
Near threatened:		52

Useful field-identification guides:
A Photographic Guide to the Birds of Peninsular Malaysia and Singapore, M. Strange & A. Jeyarajasingam. Sun Tree, 1993.

Pocket Guide to the Birds of Borneo, C. Francis & B. Smythies. WWF Malaysia, 1984.

A Photographic Guide to Birds of Peninsular Malaysia and Singapore, G. W. H. Davison & Chew Y. F. New Holland, 1995.

Useful site-guide and check-list:
A Birdwatcher's Guide to Malaysia, John Bransbury. Waymark, 1993.

Useful address:
Malaysian Nature Society
17, Jln Tanjung SD 13/2
Sri Damansara
52200 Kuala Lumpur
Malaysia
Tel: (+60) 3-6329422/6357917/6329325
Fax: (+60) 3-6358773
E-mail: mns@natsoc.po.my
Web site:
http://www.charity.org.my/msia_nature_soc

Above: In the heart of the fertile Sunda subregion, Malaysia has a high density and variety of tropical forest birds, like woodpeckers. Here a female CRIMSON-WINGED WOODPECKER (Picus puniceus) feeds on plant sap.

Above: *The* FIRE-TUFTED BARBET
*(Psilopogon pyrolophus) occurs only
in Peninsular Malaysia and on
Sumatra. In submontane rainforest
between 600 and 1500 metres it
can be locally quite common.*

Left: *Lowland rainforest in the state
of Johor.*

habitat of the tropical rainforest offers the most intriguing, challenging but also rewarding birdwatching in Malaysia, the mangroves on the west coast of the peninsula should not be overlooked. They can be surveyed well at the Kuala Selangor Nature Park; the Malaysian Nature Society runs the park and has details. For the more adventurous, the Kuala Gula mangroves further north in Perak offer some huge expanses of mangroves that hold breeding Milky Storks and many resident herons and migratory shorebirds.

East Malaysian birds have long been covered well in text and illustrations, but amazingly for many years nobody has produced a proper field identification guide to Peninsular Malaysian birds. This should be corrected shortly, however, as two major titles covering all the Malaysian birds are at present being produced.

Below: *Montane habitat near the summit of Mount Kinabalu, Sabah.*

SINGAPORE

'SURPRISING SINGAPORE' *reads a Singapore Tourist Promotion Board slogan, and when it comes to birds Singapore is indeed surprising. No other city in South-east Asia has such a stunning density of common garden birds, with Philippine Glossy Starlings, Pink-necked Pigeons, Black-naped Orioles, Olive-backed Sunbirds and many other attractive birds feeding in the flowering and fruiting trees right along busy Orchard Road. It is so obvious that even tourists comment on this extraordinary bird life. It should also be added that some residents complain of noise and pollution near trees where hundreds of mynas roost; huge congregations of migratory Barn Swallows have been known to make a nuisance of themselves at similar roosts.*

However, for the most part, the bird life of Singapore is a delight. It is probably the best place in the region to view birds of the garden, park and open country habitat. The island is also on a major migration route which means that thousands of shorebirds and also some perching birds from northern Asia pass through or spend the northern winter months here. They can be seen well in many parts of the island. Even some good South-east Asian specialities, like Jambu Fruit-dove (*Ptilinopus jambu*) and Copper-throated Sunbird (*Nectarinia calcostetha*), can be seen with more certainty and with better views in Singapore than probably anywhere else in the world!

Through the so-called 'Garden City' concept, the government has promoted the proliferation of greenery all over the city and adaptable birds have benefited from this. With regards to legislation, Singapore is a nature conservationist's dream come true: apart from six numerous or introduced bird species regarded as pests, all vertebrate animals in the republic are protected against killing and capture.

Almost every year one or more new species are added to the Singapore bird list, but these are mostly migratory or widespread species that pop up on occasions and are spotted by the growing band of sharp-eyed birdwatchers in the republic. In the meantime, many resident birds are not doing so well, especially rainforest and mangrove species.

The rapid development of Singapore has put a strain on the scarce land resources of the city state and this has led to many birds becoming locally extinct. In a study published in his book *Vanishing Birds of Singapore* (Nature Society (Singapore), 1992) local ornithologist Lim Kim Seng documented that in 1940 180 birds were resident, 35 having already become locally extinct. Since then, 39 have most likely become extinct and a further 52 are in danger of becoming extinct in the near future – mostly forest birds, but also some wetland species. This serves as a lesson to other countries in the region that are about to become successful like Singapore, except that in those countries 'locally extinct' could very well mean 'globally extinct'.

***Below:** Marsh habitat at the dammed Kranji River.*

BIRDS OF SINGAPORE AT A GLANCE

Number of species:	335
Number of endemics:	0
Number of threatened species:	6
Near threatened:	2

Useful field-identification guides:

Birds of Singapore, Lim Kim Seng. Sun Tree, 1997.

The Birds of Singapore, C. Briffett & S.B. Supari. Oxford University Press, 1993. (Includes checklist and site guide.)

A Photographic Guide to Birds of Peninsular Malaysia and Singapore, G. W. H. Davison & Chew Y. F. New Holland, 1995.

Useful address:
The Nature Society (Singapore)
601 Sims Drive, # 04-04
Singapore 387382
Tel: (+65) 741 2036
Fax: (+65) 741 0871

Singapore is one of the best places in the world to see the rare CHINESE EGRET (Egretta eulophotes), which breeds in China and Korea but spends the northern winter in South-east Asia. During this period it is so similar in appearance to the Reef Egret (Egretta sacra) that even the experts make mistakes and collected skins have been known to be wrongly identified in museums. So why is the Chinese Egret rare and globally endangered with extinction when the Reef Egret is so common throughout the region? It is probably because it is too specialized: the Chinese Egret is apparently unable to adapt to any habitat other than a narrow strip of undisturbed tidal mudflat – fortunately this happens to be available in Singapore.

Above: Birding at Pulau Ubin off the main island.

Right: A skilful core of birdwatchers keep track of Singapore's bird life and each year new species are added to the republic's list. Most are rare vagrants like this juvenile HIMALAYAN GRIFFON (Gyps himalayensis) which turned up in 1992 together with eight compatriots. This was the first time this species had been recorded on the Malay Peninsula, 3,000 kilometres outside its regular range.

Below: Rainforest on Mindanao which has the most forest cover of all the Philippine islands.

Pete Morris

THE PHILIPPINES

IN ZOOGEOGRAPHICAL TERMS *the Philippines lie at the fringes of the Oriental region. This means that the typical Oriental families of cuckoos, kingfishers, cuckoo-shrikes, babblers, bulbuls, flycatchers, sunbirds and flowerpeckers are all well represented; but you also find many migrants from the Eastern Palaearctic region which is close by to the north, and some families, like pigeons and parrots, related more to the Australasian region to the south. The most significant fact, however, is that 45 per cent of all Philippine resident land birds are endemic to that country.*

Pete Morris

Right: This rare photograph shows a BLUE-CAPPED WOOD-KINGFISHER (Actenoides hombroni), one of the species endemic to the Philippines. It is restricted to primary montane forest in Mindanao. There are few recent records of this species and it is listed as vulnerable to global extinction due to habitat destruction.

Virtually all the endemic birds depend largely or exclusively on the rainforest for their survival, and since the primary rainforests, which once covered practically the whole of the Philippine islands, now cover only 8 per cent or less of the area, a large proportion of the endemic birds are threatened with global extinction.

Amazingly, however, there have as yet been no extinctions. When one of the main references mentioned below, *The Birds of the Philippines*, was published in 1991 the small endemic Cebu Flowerpecker (*Dicaeum*

quadricolor) had not been observed since 1906, and since all its habitat had been cleared it was listed as extinct. Then in 1992 a scientist from Cambridge University found the bird in a 10-hectare patch of trees on Cebu island. A juvenile was also observed, indicating recent breeding. So, extinction is not always forever as conservationists claim!

A total of 16 Philippine birds are, like the Cebu Flowerpecker, regarded as being critically threatened with extinction. They include other flagship species like the Philippine Eagle, which has a

world population of probably less than 200 individuals. Most of these live in the remote forests of Sierra Madre in north-eastern Luzon, which together with the southern islands of Mindanao and Palawan is the only place with large expanses of good rainforest habitat left in the country.

In few countries has the natural habitat been devastated so quickly and so severely as it has in the Philippines. Yet it is a wonderful place to go travelling and birdwatching. The Philippine people are friendly and well educated, and for better or for

Right: Found only in the Philippines, the SPOTTED WOOD-KINGFISHER (Actenoides lindsayi) is endemic to primary and secondary rainforest in this country. It is listed as near-threatened with extinction. This is a female.

The WHITE-FRONTED TIT (Parus semilarvatus) is one of the Philippines' rare endemic species and is listed as near-threatened with extinction. It is restricted to lowland forest where it moves singly or in mixed flocks.

BIRDS OF THE PHILIPPINES AT A GLANCE

Number of species:	556
Number of endemics:	169
Number of threatened species:	70
Near threatened:	49

Useful field-identification guides:
Philippine Birds, J.E. du Pont. Delaware Museum, 1971.

Check-lists:
The Birds of the Philippines, E.C. Dickinson, R.S. Kennedy & K.C. Parkes. British Ornithologists Union, 1991.

Useful site-guides:
The Philippines: A Birders Guide, Dave Sargeant. Unpublished, 1992.

Useful address:
Haribon Foundation
340 Villamor Street, San Juan
Metro Manila
1500 Philippines
Tel: (+6-32) 784179
Fax: (+6-32) 704316
E-mail: Haribon@phil.gn.apc.org

worse, are slightly more westernized than other Asian nations thanks to the American influence. If you study the listed books well before you go and travel in a group or with a good guide you can have the birdwatching trip of a lifetime.

Right: Endemic to the Philippines and with a world population of maybe just 200 birds, the PHILIPPINE EAGLE (Pithecophaga jefferyi) is regarded as endangered with extinction.

1NDONESIA

WITH 1,531 SPECIES *on its checklist, Indonesia has one of the richer avifaunas in the world. No single country has more endemic species: 381 is the staggering number of species that can be seen only in Indonesia. Unfortunately, Indonesia holds another important world record – no country has a higher number of endangered species! In the 1994 BirdLife International list of globally threatened bird species, Indonesia came out top with 104 species (followed closely by Brazil with 103 species).*

BIRDS OF INDONESIA AT A GLANCE

Number of species:	1,531
Number of endemics:	381
Number of threatened species:	104
Data deficient:	30
Near-threatened:	152

Useful field-identification guides:
Field Guide to the Birds of Borneo, Sumatra, Java and Bali, J. MacKinnon & K. Philips. Oxford University Press, 1993.

A Guide to the Birds of Wallacea, B.J. Coates & K.D. Bishop. Dove, Australia, 1997.

Birds of New Guinea, B.M. Beehler, T.K. Prat & D.A. Zimmerman. Princeton University Press, 1986.

The Birds of Sulawesi, Derek Holmes. Oxford University Press, 1997.

A Photographic Guide to Birds of Borneo, G. W. H. Davison & Chew Y. F. New Holland, 1996.

Check-lists:
The Birds of Indonesia, Paul Andrew. Indonesian Ornithological Society, 1992.

The Birds of Wallacea, C.M.N. White & M.D. Bruce. British Ornithologist Union, 1986.

Useful site-guides:
Wallacea: A Site Guide for Birdwatchers, David Gibbs. Unpublished, 1990.

Birding Indonesia, P. Jepson & R. Ounsted. Periplus Editions, 1997.

The BLUE-AND-WHITE KINGFISHER
(Halcyon diops) is endemic to Halmahera and some nearby islands in eastern Indonesia where it is locally quite common.

Useful Addresses:
BirdLife International Indonesia Programme
Jl. Jend. A. Yani 11
PO Box 310
Bogor 16003
Indonesia
Tel/fax: (+62) 251 333234
E-mail: pj@server.indo.net.id
Web site: http://www.kt.rim.or.jp/-birdinfo/indonesia/

Indonesian Ornithological Society (publishes *Kukila*)
(same address)

The wealth of Indonesian birdlife is mainly due to the fact that the country straddles two major zoological realms: the Oriental and the Australasian regions. No single field guide covers the whole area and therefore it is advantageous to study the birds in seven smaller sections. Sumatra, Kalimantan (Indonesian Borneo) and Java/Bali have Oriental region birds, some of which are endemic but most are shared with Malaysia and southern

Right: Found only in Indonesia: The vocal BAR-WINGED PRINIA (Prinia familiaris) is a common bird in scrub and gardens in Sumatra, Java and Bali.

Above: The Bali Barat National Park during the dry season, the only location where one of the rarest birds in the world, the Bali Starling, can still be seen.

Nature Conservation (PHPA) under the Ministry of Forestry. In Eastern Indonesia especially, much work has been carried out recently surveying little-known sites in Wallacea.

New reports and field guides from these areas are produced each year. This means that there is now more information available on where to go and how to find and identify the different species. Eventually a greater understanding and appreciation of the Indonesian bird life will also lead to better protection of the birds and their habitats.

Birdwatching in Indonesia is hard work. The density of birds near populated areas is small due to hunting and excessive use of pesticides, and the birds are often quite shy. However, if you know where to go off the beaten track, or if you get a good guide to help you, the country also offers some of the best birdwatching there is, with a wealth of peculiar and colourful species that are found

Thailand. Sulawesi, Maluku and the Nusa Tengarra (collectively called Wallacea) have a mixture of Oriental and Australasian birds plus many endemics. The final section, Irian Jaya on the island of New Guinea, is part of the Australasian region proper.

Although there are still large gaps in our knowledge of Indonesian birds, these gaps are quickly being filled. Important bodies on the Indonesian birdwatching scene include the Indonesian Ornithological Society, BirdLife Indonesia, and the Directorate General of Forest Protection and

Below: Montane rainforest on Java.

ACKNOWLEDGEMENTS

It was a major step for me when, in 1986, I retired from my comfortable career as a petroleum engineer in South-east Asia. I had developed an interest in the natural environment and I felt there was an urgent need for better documentation of the little-known wildlife there, especially the birds that I have enjoyed photographing since I was a teenager.

The region was then developing economically at a breath-taking pace, in fact it still is. This is excellent and impressive. I just felt at that stage that the public lacked information on what treasures were stored in the natural world that surrounded them, a world put under heavy strain by the developments. Only a properly informed public could make qualified choices regarding the future they really wanted: fierce consumerism or a balanced development. So I started photographing birds and marketing my material, showing people that wild birds were beautiful, exciting and important. The Singaporean immigration department had the decency and trust in my abilities to approve my application for residency.

I would like to thank all those who supported me at that stage. They are too many to mention here by name but they know who they are: my friends in the Malaysian Nature Society and the Nature Society of Singapore; my companions and guides on regional travels; my first clients, the lifestyle and airline magazine editors who began printing nature articles, at first hesitantly, then later enthusiastically; guide book editors who began including nature in their books as a worthwhile visitor's attraction; the Jurong Bird Park who supported the interest in wild birds as well

Morten Strange first travelled South-east Asia as a petroleum engineer and then as a wildlife photographer, residing in Singapore from 1980 until 1993. His photographs and articles have appeared in all the major magazines and guidebooks from the region. He worked as the International Officer for DOF-BirdLife Denmark from 1994 until 1996 when he resumed his freelance work as photographer and writer specializing in South-east Asian birds and development affairs.

as captive ones; and private companies and governmental departments who began supporting birds and nature in their campaigns. Thanks to all of you.

Since then the interest in South-east Asian wildlife has virtually exploded. Every year new documentation appears and pro-green and pro-sustainable development are today viewed as something constructive and admirable.

But there is still work to be done, and I would like to thank Managing Director John Beaufoy, Publishing Manager Jo Hemmings and their staff with New Holland (Publishers) Ltd for producing this latest effort to document the magnificent bird life of South-east Asia. Also thanks to D & N Publishing who did the creative design.

Since I started my efforts, many local photographers have begun working on birds and have improved their skills quickly. Travellers from the West also produce some rare photographs, and I have been very lucky that some of my friends in that category have allowed me to use their material. For that I would especially like to thank Frank Lambert, Pete Morris, Ong Kiem Sian, Pilai Poonsward, Uthai Treesucon and Alan Ow Yong. Thank you for your invaluable contributions, I know how hard you have had to work to get such rare shots. Ng Bee Choo assisted by coordinating contact with contributors. My ornithologist friend through many years, Lim Kim Seng, read through the text to check for scientific errors, although the final version of text and pictures is entirely my own responsibility.

Further information

Apart from the titles mentioned here which cover most of South-east Asia, new material on Asian bird life is continuously being produced; each year new books appear. Look out especially for unpublished or small circulation site guides and trip reports produced by travelling birdwatchers that are often great sources of honest information and inspiration. The book services listed will have such details. When birdwatching in a new area in Asia, a local nature guide is often essential. Commercial tour companies can sometimes assist; they advertise in all birdwatching magazines. Alternatively, the societies mentioned in each country chapter will be able to recommend somebody.

Field identification guide
A Field Guide to the Birds of South-East Asia
B. King, M. Woodcock & E.C. Dickinson. Collins, 1975.

Site guide
Where to Watch Birds in Asia
Nigel Wheatley. Helm, 1996.

Checklist
An Annotated Checklist of the Birds of the Oriental Region
Inskipp, Lindsey & Duckworth. Oriental Bird Club, 1996.

Useful addresses
Birdlife International
Wellbrook Court
Girton Road
Cambridge CB3 0NA
UK
Tel: (+44) 1223 277318
Fax: (+44) 1223 277200
E-mail: birdlife@birdlife.org.uk

Oriental Bird Club
The Lodge
Sandy
Bedfordshire SG19 2DL
UK
Web site: hhtp://www.netlink.co.uk/users/aw/obchome.html

Book services:
Natural History Book Service Ltd
2–3 Wills Road
Totnes
Devon TQ9 5XN,
UK
Tel: (+44) 1803 865913
Fax: (+44) 1803 865280
Web site: http://www.nhbs.co.uk

Nature's Niche
Bukit Timah Nature Reserve Visitor Centre
177 Hindhede Drive
Singapore 589333
Tel: (+65) 4636571
Fax: (+65) 4636572
E-mail: nniche@singnet.com.sg

INDEX